PEBBLE ISLAND

Operation Prelim

The Golden Journey to Samarkand

(SAS adopted poem by James Elroy Flecker)

What shall we tell you?

Tales, marvellous tales

Of ships and stars and isles where good men rest...

PEBBLE ISLAND
Operation Prelim

FRANCIS MACKAY WITH **JON COOKSEY**

Pen & Sword
MILITARY

First published in Great Britain in 2007 by
Pen & Sword Military an imprint of
Pen & Sword Books Ltd
47 Church Street
Barnsley
South Yorkshire
S70 2AS

Copyright © Francis Mackay with Jon Cooksey, 2007

ISBN 978-1-84415-515-6

A CIP catalogue record for this book is
available from the British Library

Printed and bound in the United Kingdom by CPI

Pen & Sword Books Ltd incorporates the Imprints of Pen & Sword Aviation, Pen
& Sword Maritime, Pen & Sword Military, Wharncliffe Local History, Pen and
Sword Select, Pen and Sword Military Classics and Leo Cooper.

For a complete list of Pen & Sword titles please contact
PEN & SWORD BOOKS LIMITED
47 Church Street, Barnsley, South Yorkshire, S70 2AS, England
E-mail: enquiries@pen-and-sword.co.uk
Website: www.pen-and-sword.co.uk

CONTENTS

ACKNOWLEDGEMENTS

Thanks go to many people for their assistance with this book. In the Falklands four people were outstandingly generous with their time, patiently answering strange questions on apparently obscure matters. Roger Edwards, a former Royal Navy helicopter observer, married to a Falklands girl and farming at Fox Bay West, served throughout the Falklands campaign, mainly as Adviser, (Helicopters) Special Forces and on anything relating to the Islands. Allan White, co-proprietor with his partner, Jacqui Jennings, of the comfortable Pebble Island Lodge, a haven for bird watchers and the occasional military tourist. Raymond Evans, in 2005 manager of Pebble Island farm; who in 1982, along with his wife Olwyn and their children Russell and Tracy, endured the Argentinian occupation and is an authority on anything about the island and those troubled times. Special thanks go to Russell Evans for providing a wide selection of excellent photographs of his island home. Ken Berntsen, Allan White's uncle, provided information about the Argentinians' use of Land Rovers and other matters. Elsewhere thanks to Sam Miller, formerly of Keppel Island, for information on that island's brief contacts with war. In Stanley two people really went out of their way to be helpful; Margaret Williams, Tourism Development Co-ordinator, based at the Jetty Visitor's Centre and Colin Patterson-Smith, Assistant Manager, Falkland Islands Museum, respectively.

In the UK our gratitude is extended to Jerry Shore, and his successor, Catherine Rounsfell, Assistant Curator, Fleet Air Arm Museum, Yeovilton, Somerset; and Ian Howat, Ayrshire, for photographs of the remains of the Argentinian aircraft on Pebble Island. Squadron Leader (Retd.) Derek Crapper, MBE AE, RAFVR, rendered special assistance with the translation of documents from Argentina (and for providing the correct spelling of the word 'Bergan'!). To Lieutenant Colonel (Retd.) Keith Eve RA, an authority on Naval Gunfire Support (NGS) and one of its most experienced exponents, for generous access help. Major (Retd.) Bob Bragg, former RAF pilot and one-time Company Commander with 12/13 Bn Parachute Regiment (TA), delved deep into his copious archive on special and elite forces operations to produce images and important items of obscure information. Sandy McClearn, webmaster of www.hazegray.org, for assistance with photographs of ships and their weapons and to his MD Thomas, for permission to use them.

Many people in Argentina have been extremely supportive and co-operative. Our thanks to 'Esteban' (not his real name) whom like others, wishes to remain anonymous. However, we are able, and pleased, to acknowledge publicly the assistance provided by Emilio Duca, of the *Direccion de Estudios Historicos de la Fuerza Aerea Argentina* in Buenos Aires, especially for clarifying the fate of the 'sixth Pucara' on Pebble Island and for supplying a copy of *Separata No 2 Borbon, Equipo de Combate Marega, Gesta Malvinas 82*, one of a series within the *Revista Desembarco* journal.

Our thanks also to Jorge Gazzola, webmaster of **www.Helis.com** and **www.FuerzasNavales.com** for permission to use material and photographs regarding 2nd Helicopter Squadron operation to Pebble Island, and of course to the author of the article, Sr. Santiago Aversa.

At all times the sponsors and webmasters of the websites of the Argentinian armed forces and protective services were helpful and courteous.

Also thanks to the following for assistance as indicated. Antonio Carmo, Portugal, for information about Argentinian Special Forces and their role in the South Atlantic Campaign. Harry Pugh, Arlington, Virginia provided valuable assistance with insignia worn by Argentinian armed forces and protective services. Galen R Frysinger, Sheboygan, Wisconsin, gave permission to use photographs of locations in the Falklands as did Marcelo Ribeiro in Brazil. Whilst every effort has been made to trace the copyright holders of illustrations included in the book, where this has not been possible the publishers would be happy to hear from those affected.

Francis Mackay and Jon Cooksey

The issue of sovereignty of the Malvinas lies deep within the Argentinian psyche and their 'recovery' has haunted generations of politicians, patriots and ordinary people. As a result the Argentinian military have long planned a landing on the Falklands – and so, once, did the British. During the 1920s the Royal Navy Staff College, Greenwich, ran a paper-exercise featuring an amphibious landing on the Falklands. Nothing sinister, just a locale unfamiliar to the players but well mapped and reasonably well charted, with abundant copies of each lying to hand in an adjacent military map store. The players selected San Carlos Water as the landing site, but fortunately no Argentinian defence analyst unearthed the papers – neither did a British one until the 1990s!

In 1981 the Argentinian *Junta Militar*, three senior officers with little grasp of politics or diplomacy, were hugely unpopular with their restive people. In an attempt to regain, or, rather, to acquire, popular acclaim they decided to play the Malvinas card, and directed their high command, the *Comando Militar* (COMIL) to prepare a coup-de-main, Operation Rosario. The planning group comprised officers from all three armed services, albeit mainly from the *Armada*, *Infanteria*, CANA (naval aviation), and FAA (air force) given the nature of the intended operation; the *Ejercito Argentina* (army) was also represented. As the aim of the operation was integration (incorrectly proclaimed as 're-integration' by ardent nationalists) of the islands into Argentina, the national police and land frontier protection force, the *Gendarmerie Nacional*, (GN), and the coastguard, the *Prefectura Naval Argentina* (PNA) were also involved.

Operation ROSARIO. Landing the Landing Force, LST Cabo San Antonio at Yorke Bay, 2 April 1982. Infanteria de Marina Argentina

Infanteria de Marina and RM/FIDF surrendered personnel, Stanley. Infanteria de Marina Argentina

In early 1982, the *Junta* issued *Directiva Estrategica Nacional* 1/82, initiating the operation. The invasion fleet sailed in late March. The spearhead of the almost bloodless assault, delayed by bad weather at sea until 2 April 1982 consisted of elite teams from the *Armada* and the *Infanteria de Marina*. It was hailed by the *Junta*'s publicity aparatus as a major victory,

The British responded quickly, and starkly; one man killed and more than a hundred captured on South Georgia, whilst 321 died in an attack on the ARA *Belgrano*.

Not all responses were so brutal. On 14 May a daring British raid disabled an entire group of Argentinian aircraft without loss to either side. The raid, Operation PRELIM, was the first purely SAS airfield attack since late 1944, and possibly the largest assault mounted by the Regiment since that on the Jebel Akhdar in 1956. (Who can say what may have happened since then?) [1]

The raid was an extremely high-risk venture for the British Task Force. It imperilled most of the British transport helicopters, around one third of the Special Forces personnel, the chief Naval Gunfire Support (NGS) officer plus one of only five Naval Gunfire Forward Observers (NGFOs) in the South Atlantic and two warships. Above all, it endangered HMS *Hermes*, the Task Force's 'Mission Essential Unit' -'Lose *Hermes*, lose the war'. [2]

To launch the raid this ageing but militarily priceless helicopter carrier was deliberately deployed into an area probably patrolled by Argentinian submarines.[3] At the same time it would come within range of missile-armed aircraft which had recently sunk the first major British warship to be lost to enemy action since 1945.[4]

So why had PRELIM been mounted and why, despite the obvious risks, was it initiated by Rear Admiral Sandy Woodward, endorsed by Commodore Michael Clapp and Brigadier Julian Thompson and sanctioned by Admiral Sir John

Fieldhouse and Brigadier Peter de la Billiere? This book attempts to answer that question by describing the threat posed by an Argentinian force on Pebble Island, its elimination and the subsequent tragic events, including the loss of HMS *Coventry* and MV *Atlantic Conveyor*, both, it is argued, as a direct result of the SAS raid.

A NOTE ON TERMINOLOGY

Operation PRELIM was the code name allocated to the SAS Pebble Island raid. It was technically part of Operation SUTTON, the amphibious landings and subsequent land battle conducted as part of Operation CORPORATE, the restoration of British sovereignty of various territories in the South Atlantic.

The Argentinians call the Falkland Islands '*Islas Malvinas*'; homesick French explorers from St. Malo christened the archipelago *Iles Malouines*, in Spanish Islas Malvinas.

The *Armada Republica Argentina* (ARA - Navy) designated the Pebble Island Forward Operating Base (the airfield, garrison and fortified settlement) as either *Estacion Aeronavale Bahia Elefante* or *Base Aeronavale Calderon*. The *Fuerza Aerea Argentina* (FAA-Argentinian Air Force) preferred *Estacion Aero Calderon* or *Base Aero Militar Calderon*; sometimes *La Payanca* from the radio call sign. The *Infanteria de Marina* (Marines) used *Aerodromo de Campana* [Field] *Aeronaval de Isla de Borbon*. The soldiery simply called it Borbon; so will the authors.

In the same way the Marine garrison is variously described as the *Destacada De Cuerpo De Infanteria De Marina a Borbon; Equipo de Combate Marega; Equipo de Combate Borbon; Equipo de Combate Calderon, Equipo de Combate H Companga Batalon de Infanteria de Marina No 3 and Eq. Comb/H/BIM3*. Here it is just *Equipo Marega*.

The *Armada Republica Argentina* is rendered here as the *Armada*, and its *Cuerpo de Infanteria de Marina* as the *Infanteria*. That force has Sections, not (British 1982) Rifle or Machine Gun Groups within Sections, and Groups, not (British) Sections. Two Groups and HQ team form a 'Peleton' a Squad. A 32-man Squad could be carried by a single LVTP7 amphibious landing vehicle. The *Armada* and *Infanteria* have three subaltern ranks; Lieutenant, Sub-Lieutenant and Midshipman, all used to fill command appointments such as Squad or Supply Section commander.

To simplify the text for the reader accents have been omitted from Spanish words.

THE THREAT

Amphibious warfare operations require, amongst other things, exceptionally careful planning and accurate intelligence. Operation **ROSARIO** was no exception. The Argentinian planning staff developed an interest in Pebble Island as they reasoned it would make a useful Forward Operating Base (FOB) – not only for themselves but also for the British if they gained control.

Apart from planning the invasion the COMIL considered possible British responses, including an amphibious counter-attack; the Royal Navy certainly had the necessary experience, training and equipment. This notion was initially discounted by the *Junta*, and hence by the COMIL. However, several senior officers in the planning group, graduates of command and staff colleges at home and abroad, argued the case for contingency planning. Eventually their views were reluctantly accepted by the *Junta*, and a secret post-invasion defence plan, known as *La Planicacion de Operaciones 2/82 Mantenimiento de la Soberania*, was discretely prepared.

Some Armada officers were convinced that, given the distance between the Falklands and the UK, the British would try to establish a FOB on South Georgia or the Falklands. This 'stone frigate' could provide supply, communications and

Wideawake Airfield, Ascension Island.

maintenance sites. Also, if sited on the Falklands, it could house an airfield for air-defence and attack aircraft and helicopters in addition to a lair for raiding forces; a concept tested by NATO for the forward defence of sensitive coastal locations.

From the British point of view such a base could be used as a political bargaining chip. Island-based fighter aircraft, (Sea Harriers or RAF Phantoms), surface to air missiles, Royal Navy ship-borne Sea Dart and Sea Slug and RAF air-transportable Bloodhound could all be used to interdict Argentinian air lines of communication from the mainland while British submarines neutralised the sea lines of communication, effectively marooning the Falklands garrison. The Argentinians knew that RAF Harrier squadrons in Germany frequently exercised from dispersed hides. They also knew that Hercules squadrons habitually operated from rough airstrips around the world. And, if fitted with US-style refuelling probes for use with Victor K2 tankers, RAF Hercules could supply the FOB from Ascension Island.

FOBs ON WEST FALKLAND

Admiral Sandy Woodward.

The idea of establishing a FOB on West Falkland or an outer island occurred to at least one British officer before the landings at San Carlos. Admiral Woodward wanted to have a large airfield for Hercules transports, Phantom air-defence fighters, Harrier ground and maritime attack aircraft, and various types of helicopter.[1] A number of locations on the Falklands seemed suitable especially that of Pebble Island. The Admiral also considered establishing a special forces base on Kidney Island, close to Stanley although his advisers dissuaded him from pursuing those ideas. [2]

However, Special Boat Squadron (SBS) patrols manned observation posts (OPs) across the Falkland group during the campaign. These included Carcass Island, west of Pebble - named after a RN ship which had surveyed it in Nelson's time and aboard which Nelson had himself served in 1776 - and even the remote Weddell Island in the far south east, just in case the enemy tried to establish FOBs on them. [3]

A British FOB would pose a serious problem to the Argentinians, who also needed one on West Falkland as a radar site. Irrespective of any British counter-offensive the Argentinians intended to extend their national Airspace Surveillance and Air Traffic Control system to cover the 'reintegrated' province of the Islas Malvinas. Immediate post-invasion cover would be provided by a mobile unit, *Grupo 2 Vigilancia y Control Aereo*. It had been formed in 1980 as part of an *Escuadron Aereos Moviles*, following a period of tension, verging on transition to war, with Chile, over control of three islands in a seaway between the two nations. The highly mobile *Grupo* could ostensibly control air operations by the *Escuadron* from any location in southern Patagonia/Tierra del Fuego. However, as the Beagle Channel event took place in 1978 the *Escuadron* was probably formed with the Falklands in mind.

(Argentina laid claim to all of the huge island of Tierra del Fuego as well as the Falklands, South Georgia and the South Sandwich Islands, hence the existence of four stars on some military patches and badges.)

The *Grupo* included not only a surveillance radar unit but also a Fighter-Control Station (*Estacion de Interceptacion*, or EI) and a *Centro de Informacion y Control* (CIC). The need for radar on West Falkland became more urgent when, during planning for post-invasion defences, it became obvious that the hills to the north and west of Stanley would restrict radar reception from equipment anywhere in the town. Stanley's modest road network was the only way of moving and mounting the Argentinians' heavy US radar sets and generators. The *Grupo* was equipped with Westinghouse TPS-44 and TP-43 radar systems, each

**FAA Pucara
Squadron arm patch.**

with a range of about 150 miles. If sited around Stanley airfield the hills would restrict cover to a 10°-210° arc, and the low elevation of the only accessible sites would restrict the range to 130 miles to the north-east and east, but only 45-80 to the south due to more hills. That left an uncomfortably large sector uncovered for air-traffic control purposes and also left it open to enemy incursion. The ideal solution was to place a radar site on the north coast of West Falkland, preferably in a FOB.

In the event of a British counterstroke the FOB could be protected by mobile surface to air missiles such as the *Infanteria*'s British-built Tigercat and the FAA and *Ejercito*'s radar-controlled anti-aircraft guns. The FOB could

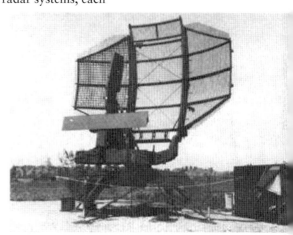

TPS 43 radar.

APPROXIMATE AREA OF RADAR SHADOW

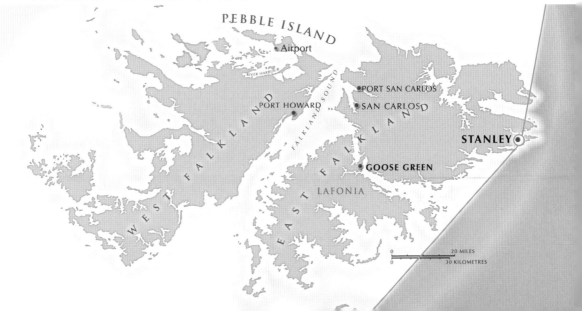

Armada Argentina *Intrepida* Class Fast Attack Craft. Armada Argentina

also have an offensive role, accommodating *Armada* Fast Attack Craft, and special forces, and light reconnaissance/attack aircraft and helicopters from all of the armed and protective services. It would, however, have to be protected by a strong garrison, covered by minefields and barbed wire entanglements and equipped with artillery, mortars and machine guns firing along fixed lines to cover beaches and possible drop zones (DZs) or helicopter landing sites (LZs). The FOB could also be sheltered by an air defence umbrella based on strengthened and lengthened runways at Stanley and covered by a surveillance radar set. Thus a FOB on the north coast of West Falkland was an attractive proposition to some Argentinian planners, although all hoped it was one which would not be required to be used.[4]

The ideal location, for Argentinian or British forces, would be a settlement with an airstrip capable of expansion to accept FAA Dagger/RAF Phantom air-defence fighters and Hercules transports. (The FAA assessed five landing sites as suitable for Hercules operations; Stanley and Goose Green on East Falkland, and Dunnose Farm, Keppel and Pebble Islands on West Falkland.) The ideal location would also need to have a pier, or at least a sheltered bay with an open beach, to enable landing craft or amphibious vehicles to land supplies. Ideally it should also possess a settlement providing a basic logistical infrastructure such as electricity, a pure water supply, shelter, telephone lines and access to fresh meat. In addition it would be close to high ground for siting radar, signals equipment and manned observation posts.

Pebble Island ticked all the boxes required by both sides. The Argentinians therefore decided that once Operation ROSARIO was complete, Pebble Island should be occupied as a matter of urgency.

PEBBLE ISLAND

The Falkland Islands lie some four hundred miles east of Argentina, and eight thousand south of the United Kingdom. There are two very large islands, West and East Falkland, and 200 smaller ones; in 1982 they had about 1200 inhabitants in a handful of settlements and thousands of sheep and penguins. Falkland Islanders proudly – and justifiably – claim that their home is 'Green, Clean, and Serene', but for ten weeks in 1982 parts, such as Pebble Island, were not entirely green, and very far from clean or serene.

Pebble Island, *Isla Borbon* to Argentinians, lies off the north coast of West Falkland. It is separated from its large neighbour in the east by a couple of narrow channels, the Tamar and Inner Passes and in the south by Pebble and Keppel Sounds. The island measures twenty-four miles by three, but less than one at its 'waist', which is also the site of the only settlement, 'Pebble' to Islanders, 'Calderon' to Argentinians. It is dominated by First Mountain, one of three hills on the island's western half. Elsewhere Pebble Island is girded by cliffs, bluffs and a few beaches. Elephant Beach, a four mile long stretch just north of the settlement in the bay of the same name, is the longest in the Falklands. It abounds with the smooth red and yellow semi-translucent stones which gave the island its name and forms the basic raw material for some fine local jewellery. To the rear of

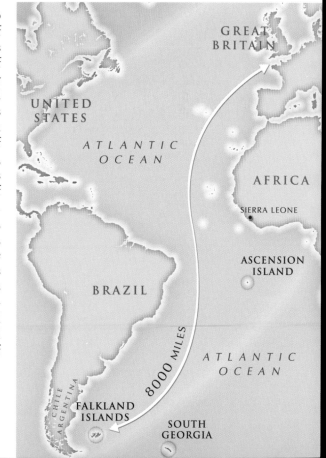

PEBBLE ISLAND

FALKLAND SOUND

WEST FALKLAND

EAST FALKLAND

• SAN CARLOS

STANLEY •

**PEBBLE ISLAND
LOCATION**

SOUTH ATLANTIC OCEAN

Jenesta Point

PEBBLE ISLAND

Wreck Point

NORTH
FALKLAND
SOUND

FIRST MOUNTAIN

VICTOR CREEK

Little Wreck Point

MARKHAM VALLEY

CLIPPING VALLEY

ELEPHANT
BAY

KEPPEL SOUND

Airfield

Pebble Island Settlement

PADDOCKS
& PARKS

SHAG ROCKS

BROKEN ISLAND

Sturgess Point

PHILLIPS COVE

Elephant Beach is an area of dunes known as the Sand Hills.

East of the beach lie important wildlife breeding grounds in a large expanse of ponds and marshes, watered by streams draining a low, undulating plateau, which extends as far as the southern coast and is given over to sheep runs. These latter are subdivided by wire and batten fences and the only stone wall on the island, built years ago to create a lambing pen. The wall extends from the settlement to the coast near Fish Creek and is described as being, 'about five feet high

The Pebble Island settlement and airfield. R Evans

and two wide, built from stones dug from vegetable plots over the years. Quite an obstacle to anyone in a hurry.' Peat fires are a feature of Falklands life and the diggings can be dangerous to the unwary either at night or in thick mist.

After nearly two hundred years of intense cattle and sheep grazing there is little ground cover to be found on the Falklands and Pebble is no exception. There are tracts of a low, thick bush called 'diddle-dee', a source of edible berries but useless for concealing even a prone man. However, Tall Fern, a thickly leaved plant which can reach up to five feet in height, grows on the upper slopes of the island's hills,

Keppel Island Sound from First Mountain. Alan White

Elephant Beach, ponds, marshes and the plateau seen from First Mountain. Tamar Pass can be seen in the distance. Allan White

especially on First Mountain, the summit of which provides observation of much of the surrounding area.

In 1982, Pebble settlement consisted of twenty-one buildings, including a new school, a carpenter's shop, several huts, a cow shed and five dwellings each with detached gardens. These were, and still are, surrounded by shelterbelts made from chicken-wire thickened by small trees and gorse. There were also several kennels for sheep dogs. Writing in 2005, Allan White, now co-proprietor with his wife Jacqui of the Pebble Island Lodge, observed that the dogs are still,

> 'a big part of farm life in the Falklands. They are 100% working animals kept outside in kennels …several times a year there are sheep dog trials in which farmers/shepherds compete quite fiercely. These are always popular with spectators.'

By late April 1982, Pebble settlement housed seven families and one single person; a total of nineteen residents plus three evacuees from Fox Bay on West Falkland, recently occupied by Argentinian troops. The farm manager's residence, the 'Big House', was home to Griff Evans and his wife Gladys who lived there with their son Raymond, his wife Olwyn and their children, Russell and Tracey. The Big House was aptly named. It had eight bedrooms as it sometimes doubled as a guesthouse for representatives of the owners, Dean Bros. Ltd of Bradford in Yorkshire, visiting wool-buyers, Falkland Island

'Big House'.

Elephant Beach. Allan White

Government officials and itinerant workers.

Most buildings had field-stone foundations, wooden frames clad with flat-iron sheets, and corrugated-iron roofs. The only stone building was a disused blacksmith's shop by the shore, replaced in 1974 by a modern workshop. This had been erected next to the largest building on the island, the shearing shed; a robust structure with a concrete floor but unheated, draughty, and with only a single toilet draining into the settlement's septic-tank sewage system.

It is still used once a year for sheep clipping, and then for storage of the fleeces prior to shipment to Europe.

Cargo and vehicles are moved around the Falklands by small coasting vessels. Pebble has

Main Pier with MV Monsunen sailing out of the mist. R Evans

two piers; one very small and used in recent years only by small boats. Near it is the wreck of a schooner, the *Karina Kirsen*, beached in 1912 after being condemned but still visible. The other, larger pier earns the settlement a ranking as a Falkland Islands Government Class 'B' Port; that is having twelve feet of water at half-tide, allowing 250-ton ships to berth alongside. The approach to the pier head is tricky but well

The Pebble Island settlement showing gardens, shelter-belts and kennels.

Ejercito Argentina field kitchen trailer in the Falklands.

within the scope of an experienced coxswain of a naval landing craft. In the 1980s the island was served by either the Falkland Islands Company-owned MV *Monsunen* or the Falkland Islands Goverment MV *Forrest* which doubled as a coastal supply vessel and Royal Marine transport. Both vessels were fitted with simple derricks for loading and unloading items such as wool bales or fuel drums on and off tractor-drawn farm trailers. Vehicles use simple ramps. The vessels could therefore carry the Argentinian Army's German-made field kitchen trailers and other light vehicles such as jeeps and OTO-Melara 105mm Pack howitzers, assembled or broken-down into mule or trailer loads. (Argentina, like other Andean nations, has a force of well-equipped mountain troops. In 1982 some served on East Falkland.) Elephant Bay can provide sheltered anchorage for medium-sized ships. It is navigable by landing ships despite a wreck and large beds of kelp.

KELP

This is best described as a form of seaweed. It is found in abundance around the Falklands, growing on submerged rocks and wrecks.

It is a useful navigation aid as it grows most densely in shallow water and its presence indicates rocks or other underwater obstacles. It has long fronds filled with air bladders so the upper strands float on the surface. At night it shimmers in moon, or even star, light and can be seen from small craft such as rubber assault boats or canoes, providing a useful indication of the tidal flow and depth of water.

Note. Falkland tidal flows are at times subject to local peculiarities, are unique and not fully understood. All tides can be reversed by strong and prolonged winds [such as those experienced in mid-May 1982. Ed]. This can create an anomaly, reported by Islanders, that makes it not unknown for the greatest range of tides, (usually associated with springs) to occur up to five days after the full or new moon. This effect is unpredictable and unexplained.[1]

The two Sounds, and Elephant Bay, and many other Falkland coastal areas, have been carefully surveyed over the years and the results published in Admiralty charts.

COASTAL SURVEY

by Roger Edwards now a resident of Fox Bay West, whom, in 1973-75, served aboard HMS *Endurance* in the South Atlantic as a Fleet Air Arm Helicopter Observer.

The Hydrographic Branch of the Royal Navy has supervised extensive surveys of those waters. Part of HMS *Endurance*'s [Antarctic support ship] job was to survey the Falklands. Each season a Boat Party was landed to conduct surveys, including recording tidal information. In addition there were automatic recording devices at various sites. Jack Sollis, who for many years captained the MV *Forrest,* kept meticulous notes; these were actually the basis of a guide, published as *In Falklands Islands Waters,* by Major Ewen Southby-Tailyour, Royal Marines, based on his surveys while commanding the Falklands Royal Marine garrison from 1978-79. When *Endurance* was surveying offshore Jack was employed as a local pilot.

Inter-island passenger travel is mainly by aircraft of the Falkland Islands Government Air Service (FIGAS). The template for FIGAS was the Canadian 'bush' airlines and had been formed in 1949 by the then Governor who had had recent experience of the Candian model in Ontario. The Falklands version started with war-surplus Auster Air OP light aircraft, which carried a pilot, two passengers and some mailbags from grass airstrips. They revolutionised inter-island travel but carried only a tiny payload and were uncomfortable and difficult to board, especially by sick or pregnant passengers. In 1972 two Canadian DHC-2 Beaver floatplanes were bought, capable of serving places without airstrips. In 1979 the Beavers were supplemented, then supplanted, by Britten-Norman BN2 Islander eight/nine seat landplanes; economical, sturdy and swift, they cover the seventy-five mile trip to Stanley in forty minutes.

FIGAS Islander.

In 1982 FIGAS served forty-two locations from its base near Stanley, many with several landing places. Pebble Island had six, two in use

FIRST MOUNTAIN

ELEPHANT BAY

BIG POND

LONG POND

and four more usable by an innovative military force in a war situation. (The airfield is twenty-five miles by air from San Carlos Water.)

Of the four grass strips on the settlement airfield, two -

A. 1750 ft (the main airstrip; 310°/130°)
B. 1250 ft were in use:

and two -

C. 750 ft
D. 750 ft - were disused

Two others could be utilised:

E. Elephant Beach; used in winter when the grass strips were water-logged or frozen; usable by a C130 Hercules.

F. Big Pond, near Elephant Bay, originally used by Beavers; passengers embarked and disembarked from a short pier on the west bank.

The airfield area lies on a plateau north of, and about two hundred yards from the settlement and is thirty yards higher. It would make a good DZ for paratroops and supplies, both conventional or via Low Altitude Parachute Extraction. In 1982 it also contained a small cemetery and a water tank, built on stilts and fed from a spring on the lower slopes of First

AIRFIELD LAYOUT

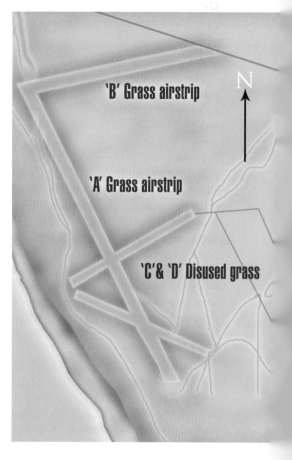

'B' Grass airstrip

N

'A' Grass airstrip

'C' & 'D' Disused grass

GRASS AIRSTRIP

PEBBLE ISLAND SETTLEMENT

Overview of the airfield area. Allan White

Mountain. The water was piped from the tank to the settlement; a simple supply, perfectly adequate for a small community swollen only during annual sheep shearing and less frequent sheepdog trials.

The various springs on the Island are fed by good rainfall throughout the year; autumn weather can best be described as squally in the morning, settling to calm, almost perfect evenings.

Pebble airfield has never had landing aids or refuelling facilities. The introduction of Islanders was followed by the arrival of a trailer-mounted, fire-pump which also provided the settlement with a much needed fire-fighting capability, given wooden-framed houses and (at times) large quantities of greasy wool in the Shearing Shed. The pump was kept in a small hut on the airfield, and a Fire Officer from Stanley trained the locals to act as a volunteer fire crew.

Some men were also trained as volunteer soldiers. They could become members of the Settlements Volunteers, one of three military formations on the Islands at the time of the Argentinian invasion. The others were the regular British Garrison known as Naval Party (NP)8901 and the Falkland Islands Defence

Fire tender hut and water tank, 2005. R Evans

Force (FIDF). NP8901 was manned by Royal Marine and Royal Navy personnel, amounting to a strong - 40 men- infantry platoon, commanded by a Major, assisted by a Subaltern and senior NCOs. The FIDF was a Territorial Army-type formation based in a Drill Hall in Stanley and equipped with small arms. The Settlements Volunteers were residents of remote communities who could be called upon to act as coast-watchers and observers during times of tension, transition to war and war. They were trained by Royal Marines touring the islands on MV *Forrest* to inspect possible landing sites. The Volunteers' training included small arms handling and shooting, including simple sniping techniques, radio handling and procedures and observation, concealment and tactical movement across all types of island terrain.

For decades Pebble Island was unknown to all but avid naturalists, Bradford wool merchants, the RN Hydrographic Branch and naval personnel serving with NP8901. There were, however, a few Argetinians who knew not only the island's name and location, but also had knowledge of its terrain and airfields.

FALKLANDS
PEBBLE ISLAND

OCCUPATION

Within a very short time of the Argentinian landings in the early hours of 2 April 1982 at Mullet Creek and Yorke Bay near Stanley, every Islander - alerted by radio - knew about them although a warning had been broadcast by the Governor, Rex Hunt, the previous day. The Falkland Islanders realised that their quiet little world, in some ways similar to Tolkein's Shire, would never be the same again. Much changed with the arrival of the Argentinians, including contact between settlements.

INTER-ISLAND CONTACT
by Roger Edwards
In 1982 Pebble Islanders had been in constant communication with the rest of the Falklands population by radio.

'There was an HF radio system [*using Associated Electrical & Lighting Ltd (AEL) equipment*], known as the 'Farmyard net', operating on 4.5 Mc/s. There was a control room in Stanley which had 24 hour cover listening-out on this frequency; islanders could even be linked into international telephone calls.

In addition many people owned 2 Metre sets operating on FM 145.5 which they used to chat between islands and settlements. These were all collected up by the Argies soon after the invasion but the AEL was given back so that people could contact the Doctor etc. in emergencies. (Doctor's hour was a very public consultation each morning at about 9 o'clock). On Pebble, Olwyn Evans had a Ham radio set but it was not set up during the conflict.'

On 9 April the change was emphasised when an English-speaking Argentinian broadcast the following message over the Farmyard Net.

'*By order of Mario Benjamin Menendez, Brigadier-General, Military Governor of the Malvinas, South Georgia, and South Sandwich Islands, with effect from 8am of the 10th April 1982, the public radio-telephone service will operate exclusively for medical emergencies; all transmissions of any [other] nature being prohibited. The military authorities, in particular the Military Police, will supervise the observance of this proclamation, and will detain without further formalities anyone who commits an infringement or possible infringement, with immediate confiscation of all material and equipment used in the said infringement.'*

Nothing much happened on Pebble Island for nearly two weeks after the announcement, apart from the appearance, on 10 April, of a strange, twin-engine aeroplane, of a type unfamiliar to the Islanders, which flew around the airfield. It was an Argentinian CANA naval aviation Tracker, inspecting the airstrips and Elephant Beach, and making some trial approach and departure runs.

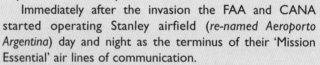

AN ARGENTINIAN FOB - BUT WHERE?

Following the invasion, the problem facing the Argentinians was finding a suitable base outside the small and soon overcrowded main airport at Port Stanley.

Immediately after the invasion the FAA and CANA started operating Stanley airfield (*re-named Aeroporto Argentina*) day and night as the terminus of their 'Mission Essential' air lines of communication.

LADE Hangar, Aeroporto Argentina in Stanley.

The relatively small airfield was always kept busy with frequent arrivals and departures of military and civil transport aircraft and helicopters. Space for loading, servicing or parking was severely limited. The first CANA and FAA officers to arrive on the islands (on 2 April) quickly rifled the FIGAS records to obtain up-to-date information on all Falkland landing sites in preparation for a carefully planned and organised aerial survey. Among the first inbound flights were two CANA S2F Trackers, deployed from helping to protect surface ships from British submarines. They were to conduct the aerial survey of the FIGAS sites and started work the following day, 3 April. Despite some delays due to poor weather the survey was completed in ten days.

Pebble Island was the ideal site for an Argentinian FOB. It had several airstrips, most of which were capable of expansion, a settlement with numerous sturdy buildings, including a mechanic's workshop, a carpenter's shop and a good pier and was near a wide beach with firm ground and relatively good exits for vehicles through the Sand Hills. The airstrips could be extended to accommodate larger aircraft and the beach could be cleared of piles of Drift Kelp; the Argentinians had experienced airfield construction teams, with mobile earth-moving equipment and pierced-steel

planking on the mainland. The Armada's Troop Landing Ship *Cabo San Antonio* could land them by LARC-5s onto Elephant Beach to enable them to build tracks through the Sand Hills to the airfield. The Landing Ship could also land radar

The Armada's Troop Landing ship the ARA Cabo San Antonio.

sets, heavy weapons and bulky defence stores such as barbed wire and corrugated iron.

On the morning of 23 April, the Pebble Islanders were alerted by a message from a (former) FIG operator in Stanley to man the Airfield Fire Trailer. There was nothing unusual in that request; a mail flight was long overdue. The operator, however, did not chat in the familiar Falklands way. He ended the transmission rather abruptly as there was an Argentinian 'minder' sitting alongside him. This was one of several enigmatic security men working for the Army Representative on the Governor's Military Intelligence Committee, Major Dowling y Palaveratti who was later to acquire an unsavoury reputation among the Islanders.

The wording of the proclamation worried the islanders and they waited apprehensively for the mail plane. A few hours later they heard the sound of an approaching Islander plane, about the only aircraft many had ever seen or heard apart from distant glimpses of passenger planes and the Argentinian Tracker, flying overhead across Pebble or around Keppel Island. The Islander landed and taxied to the Fire Trailer Hut, where most of the islanders had gathered. When the engines stopped an unfamiliar pilot emerged from the aircraft. This was Captain Felix Anselmi, a CANA pilot and he indicated to the islanders that there was mail for them to unload from the cabin. There were three other people on the aircraft. Two were familiar to the Pebble folk - Falkland Islanders, travelling to Roy Cove – but the third was another mystery man. This person, who also acted as co-pilot, was clad in an odd-looking, dark blue one-piece garment (FIGAS pilots did not wear uniforms in those leisurely days). This was a flying suit, a 'gro-bag' to the irreverent but normal garb for military aircrew everywhere. Ignoring the islanders the stranger walked along each of the grass landing strips, studying a folded chart. As he paced slowly along the grass he occasionally tested the surface by stamping down hard with a foot, especially near the thresholds and worn sections. The islanders had recently laid field drains under the 310º/130º airstrip, which lay close to the spring and could be soggy in wet weather. The 'inspector' was a CANA naval pilot and he spoke good English when asking some polite questions about the airfield. Like most of the invasion force, he and Captain Anselmi, were taken aback by the simplicity of the Falkland way of life, the fact that the islanders did not speak Spanish and that they were far from being overawed by the presence of a military officer. He made some notes on the chart and carefully studied First Mountain and the location of the water-tank. He then rejoined the other people in the Islander, which promptly took off and continued on its inter-island run.

The Pebble Islanders returned to their homes but slowly gravitated to the Big House to discuss the strange visit and to ponder on what might happen next. They had not long to wait.

Shortly after noon, some four hundred miles from Pebble Island, a CANA Beechcraft B-200 KingAir communications aircraft left BAN Rio Grande, bound for Stanley. It was carrying Captain Hector Martini, commanding officer of GAI, which would be the parent formation of the new CANA base on Pebble Island. His task was to assess the requirements of the airfield and the settlement in terms of supplies, aircraft support facilities, equipment and accommodation for possible protracted use by a detachment of aircraft, air and groundcrew and marines. If, after a fly-by and some trial approaches, he was satisfied with the airfield's suitability, he would fly on to Stanley. There he would transfer to a helicopter and return to Pebble Island for a more detailed ground survey with two other pilots. Lieutenant (Marine) Jorge Daniel Marquardt, second in command of an Amphibious Engineer Company and two combat engineers. Sergeant Juan Oviedo and *Cabo Prepales* (First Corporal) Elbio Lujan would then join the naval airmen. Their remit was to evaluate the requirements for defence works and other field engineering tasks to the airstrips and pier. The group would be escorted by a patrol of eight Marine Commandos under Sergeant Miguel Basualdo, who would also make a rough plan of ground defences for the airfield area.

The results of the fly-by were satisfactory and the King Air landed at Stanley where Captain Martini was met by Captains Moeremons and Anselmi. After a brief discussion in a hangar, at 1600hrs the three officers joined the Marines on board a *Prefectura Naval Argentina* (PNA) Puma helicopter, the only one available at that time.

PREFECTURA NAVAL ARGENTINA – THE PNA

To protect the 15,000 mile coastline of the new province and at some stage those of South Georgia and the South Sandwich Islands, the PNA organised a new sub-division, the *Prefectura Islas Malvinas* (PIM). It was commanded by *Prefecto* Ernesto Vittorello and manned by twenty coastguards ardent volunteers from PNA units on Tierra del Fuego. They were all experienced in patrolling rugged and lonely coastlines and in supplying remote coastguard stations by air or sea. The PIM consisted of a HQ, two patrol boats (*Rio Iguazu* and *Islas Malvinas*), a clearance diver, a Special Forces security team from the *Agrupacion Albatros*, and an aviation unit, the *Agrupacion Aerea Malvinas*. This was equipped with two British-built Shorts SC7 Skyvans, and a long-range French manufactured Aerospatiale Puma

Search and Rescue helicopter; both types being fitted with weather-avoidance radar. The Skyvans could carry twenty passengers in fold-down seats, and was fitted out for use by parachute rescue teams.

None of the aircraft survived. Skyvans PA-54 and 50 arrived on 21 and 30 April respectively and were used immediately to supply outlying garrisons. On 6 May PA-54 was badly damaged at Stanley by British bombs. The Puma, PA-12, arrived on 16 April and was lost on 9 May during an SAS-directed airstrike. Skyvan PA-50 was destroyed by the SAS on Pebble Island on 15 May.

All PIM personnel were awarded the *Medalla Operaciones En Combate* and *Medalla Prefectura en Malvinas*.

Patrol Boat the Rio Igazu.

Left: PNA Skyvan PA-54, badly damaged by British bombs in Stanley, 9 May 1982.

Below: PNA Skyvan PA-50 which was destroyed by the SAS on Pebble Island 15 May 1982.

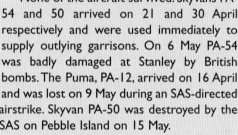

The Puma flew to San Carlos airstrip (which, after a brief fly-by, was finally rejected) before flying on to Pebble Island. It approached the settlement from the north, over Elephant Bay, and landed at the top of the slope above the settlement, about 200 yards from the Big House. The Fire Trailer was not manned; there had been no telephone call about the flight. There was therefore no one at the airstrip although most of the islanders were observing events through the windows of their homes.

The heavily-armed marines jumped out and, crouching under the spinning rotors in a well-practised drill, ran clear of the down-drafts and lay down in a rough circle, weapons at the ready. The engine was switched off and the officers and aircrew disembarked, led by Captain Moeremons. The marines stood up and, facing inwards but with two watching the settlement, formed a circle with the aircrew and survey team. Cabo Lujan planted a pole adorned with the light blue and white Argentinian flag at the top of the slope above the settlement; everyone saluted or presented arms and sang all nine verses of their national anthem *Marcha de la Patria* (March of the Fatherland). Afterwards the senior officer made a brief speech.

Captain Moeremans then walked down to the Big House and made contact with what one Argentinian account describes as '*el Administrador, Griffith Evans*'. The Captain, who spoke good English, briefed 'Griff' on the Argentinians' intentions for the airfield and settlement, and requested that all radio transmitters and weapons of any kind be handed over immediately. Griff pointed out to him that the wording of the Proclamation, as announced over the Farmyard Net, negated the radio part of that requirement, and asked if the rules had changed. The Captain appeared perplexed, and changed the subject. He stated that the Military Government of the Malvinas would send a patrol to Pebble Island from time to time, but otherwise the islanders would be cut off from the outside world. That upset and worried the listening islanders as it seemed they would have no means of getting food, or have the settlement medical chest replenished. Especially worried was Nobby Clarke and his pregnant wife Fiona; what about medical evacuation in case of an emergency? It seemed the radioed Proclamation meant nothing.

In the end it was decided to leave the radio sets in place for humanitarian reasons. Captain Moeremans made no rejoinder to any comment or requests made by the islanders; he seemed quite out of his depth, but remained at all times polite. He did not respond to questions about supplies of food, medicines or fuel for the electricity generators.

> '*There was a total of three generators on Pebble Island at the time of the conflict*', recalled Roger Edwards, '*one at the Big House where everybody was locked up after the raid, one big set for the settlement and one small one for the workshop. I did not know the size of each but probably 5KW, 15KW and 2.5KW respectively.*'

While Griff and the Captain were talking, Captains Anselmi and Martini walked the airstrips, studied their approaches and examined the Fire Tender Hut before scrutinising the settlement's buildings, the pier and the immediate area around the airstrip, making notes and sketches. Sergeant Basualdo and his young NCOs and marines patrolled the settlement and its approaches, including the pier, while the two combat engineers made some notes on defensive demolitions. After about an hour on the ground the three pilots had decided that Pebble Island airfield and settlement would make a useful FOB so the party re-entered the helicopter and returned to Stanley.

Marine Amphibious Engineer Company badge.

The next day, 24 April, the Argentinian Command in Stanley formed a new field engineering detachment, the *Grupo Ingenieros a Borbon* (GIB). It was manned by selected Army and Marine personnel from the *Agrupacion Ingenieros Malvinas*, which consisted of the *Ejercito's* 10 and 601 Engineer Companies, and the Marine Amphibious Engineer Company. The GIB consisted of a section each from Army 10th, and the Amphibious Companies; twenty-two all ranks, commanded by Lieutenant Marquardt. That afternoon a PNA Skyvan flew the GIB to Pebble Island in two 30-minute flights. The first carried Lieutenant Marquardt, four Marine and ten Army Combat Engineers plus Sergeant Basualdo and three Marine Commandos. The Lieutenant took a PRC-4031 radio set to communicate with the HQ in Stanley. On arrival the group unloaded the Skyvan which then returned to Stanley for the second load of troops and supplies. The first group established themselves, with some dismay, in the Shearing Shed, fortunately empty of fleeces. The Engineers re-erected the national flag (which appeared to have been blown over by the wind) on the edge of the airfield, and also mounted a *manga de viento*, windsock, before a quick lunch of 'C' rations.

After that the Engineers started to sort out their stores while Sergeant Basualdo and his marines approached Griff Evans. They solicited the use of a Land Rover with a full tank of fuel; he would have used the expression 'requisitioned'! They also obtained a collection of maps of various scales, selecting some at 1:25,000 because of the detailed cartography, and drove off up the slope to the airfield, following the Marble Shanty track past Middle and Marble Mountains. They were to select sites for OPs and bunkers to cover possible landing sites for enemy helicopters, amphibious vehicles, landing craft, or assault boats. They also had to search for signs of enemy recce parties, British, FIDF or Volunteers.

They stopped at the head of Clipping Valley and carefully studied the terrain, considering what they would do if they were going to raid the airfield. Sergeant Busualdo assessed that the small stony beach at the mouth of Clipping Valley would make a good landing site for 'commandos in assault craft'. It provided *cubiertas contra fuego y las vistas* (cover from fire and sight), from OPs and sentries on the airfield or in the

A new Marble Shanty alongside the old red brick one which was searched by the Argentinians. Allan White

settlement. The Marines then continued along the track to Marble Shanty (in reality two corrugated iron buildings) where they found beds and signs of cooking; not recent and not military rations but household tinned food. The patrol then explored the beach opposite Pebble Islet but did not find any evidence of enemy forces. They noted that the entire area west of the settlement was criss-crossed with fences and gullies, many not noted on the map. The patrol returned by way of Elephant Beach, the Sand Hills and the north approaches to the airfield and the settlement. There was insufficient time to reconnoitre the eastern end of the island. (After the Marines returned to Stanley Sergeant Basualdo, a man with some initiative, arranged for *Cabo Prepales* Juan Carrasco to make copies of an amended map on the photocopier at the main Argentinian HQ. One copy went to the Command Post of GRUIMVINAS, the US-style acronym for the Malvinas Marine Group, in Stanley, others went to the Amphibious Commandos and the Agrupacion *Ingenieros Malvinas*; one returned to Pebble Island.)

At 1600hrs, the Skyvan had returned. It delivered 400kgs of explosives, rations for twenty-four men for twenty days, the remainder of the Combat Engineer section, and a rather bewildered medical orderly. This was *Cabo Prepales Enfermero* Gerardo Gallio, newly arrived from the mainland and wearing only barrack, not combat, uniform. The explosives were stored in an empty house, referred to by some Argentinians as the 'School House', a name not used by the islanders (and not the new school), which had a concrete floor.

Once the whole Argentinian force was ashore on the Falklands the Argentinians activated the *Comando Conjuncto Malvinas*, (CCM), headed by the Military Governor, General Mario Menendez. As Governor the General had the last word in all matters, civil and military, having sought, if not always taken, advice from his service experts. He could, of course, be over-ruled by his political masters. To complicate matters even more in his case, one or other of the three members of the *Junta*, who were *de facto* if not *de jure* head of their respective services, at times ordered individuals, detachments and units to the Islands without informing or consulting each other or anyone else.

Command and control of a single headquarters in times of tension, transition to war and during war or warlike operations is difficult in a permanent facility and for a staff who have, mainly, trained and worked together in peacetime. The staff of the CCM had not only to learn to live with itself but co-operate and survive in makeshift premises (the former Governor's house and some requisitioned buildings) and to

Government House, post 1982.

conduct an air, land and sea war on its doorstep while almost, but never quite, cut-off from supplies.

The CCM controlled, or least attempted to control, an almost bewildering number of subordinate groups. These included Grupo 2, with the renamed *Centro de Información y Control Malvinas*. It received data not only from the two TP radars sited near Stanley, but also from several other sets. These were a single short-range Israeli-built ELTA air and ground surveillance radar, and several Skyguard fire-control sets associated with *Ejercito* short-range Roland surface to air missiles and anti-aircraft guns. They worked closely with an FAA Airfield Defence Group covering *Aeroporto Argentina*/BAM Malvinas, otherwise Stanley airport. The TP sets could not be moved to better positions due to lack of roads outside Stanley. The invasion force lacked earth-moving equipment to prepare tracks, alternate sites, and berms for protection from bomb-blast and shrapnel. Until it could be covered from West Falkland the huge area in radar shadow was the Argentinians' Achilles Heel. It was soon identified and exploited by the British, only to be countered in turn by the Argentinians' innovative use of light aircraft and observers.

ELTA coastal and airfield surveillance radar.

MANNED OBSERVATION POSTS (OPs)

The FAA knew all about manned OPs, similar to those used in Britain during the Second World War by the Royal Observer Corps, (ROC), and by similar German and Quisling organisations in occupied Europe. The *Armada* knew that coastal OPs were also used to great effect by the Norwegian section of the Special Operations Executive and by Australian Coast Watchers in the Pacific islands, to plot the movement of enemy shipping. Manned OPs have long been redundant in many nations but not Argentina, as will be recounted and some Argentinians thought the RAF still used them. They were aware that the RAF sponsored, or at least provided assistance to, the post-war ROC, which was known to man several hundred posts around the UK. (Not for observing aircraft, although the ROC maintained a well-publicised involvement in Aircraft Recognition.) There was also a precedent for wartime coast-watching (described later) in the Falklands, including Pebble Island, by the Settlements Volunteers. That was common knowledge in the islands, and probably known to inquisitive Argentinians working and living in Stanley.

When the British counter-invasion threat materialised at least one FAA officer allegedly thought the RAF would mobilise 'observers' to man OPs around any bridgehead - shades of ROC personnel on Allied ships off the Normandy beaches in 1944!

The British, however, as will be recounted later, intended using observers of a different type.

By late April early / May 1982 the three British Task Groups were heading south from Ascension Island after a final shakedown. Time was not with them. The seas around the Falklands can be difficult, even in mid-autumn. Admiral Fieldhouse in Britain, and Admiral Sandy Woodward, at sea with the three Task Groups, had much to be concerned about.

Time, however, was with the Argentinians; given enough of a breathing space they could make the Falklands impregnable. When the British started to head south with obvious malice aforethought the nascent Argentinian interest in establishing a Forward Operating Base

The radar equipped Lockheed SP-2H Neptune aircraft.

developed into something more urgent. Lacking long range aircraft the FAA used 'Aircraft Taken Up From Trade', Boeing 707 airliners, to search for the advancing British fleet. As the British force approached the Falklands the *Armada*'s four land-based radar-equipped Lockheed SP-2H Neptune aircraft flew medium-range search missions. They were, however, running out of airframe hours, so were initially restricted to anti-submarine search missions to counter British submarine operations. The Neptunes covered the *Armada*'s elderly British-built aircraft carrier the *Veinticinco de Mayo* and her escorts. The former HMS *Venerable* carried CANA A4 Skyhawk fighter-bombers and S2F Tracker anti-submarine and maritime reconnaissance aircraft. The carrier was slow and very noisy so was at considerable risk from British submarines and with good reason; one RN submarine commander reportedly said afterwards, '*I would have sailed up wet wallpaper to sink that carrier.*'

Aircraft carrier ARA Veinticinco de Mayo.

CANA A-4 SKYHAWK FIGHTER-BOMBER

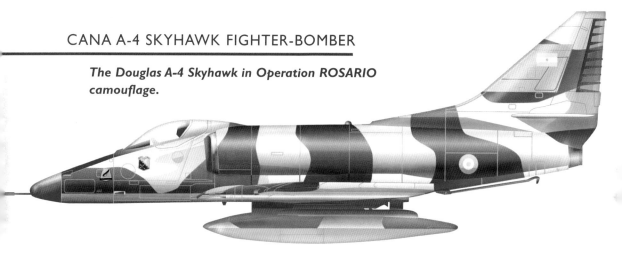

The Douglas A-4 Skyhawk in Operation ROSARIO camouflage.

BEECHCRAFT T-34C TURBO MENTOR

A T-34C Turbo Mentor, used for inshore reconnaissance.

Illustrations by Jon Wilkinson

The *Armada* could not locate and shadow the British ships with submarines. The *Fuerza de Submarinos* possessed only four boats; two former American *Guppy* class diesel-powered hunter-killers, the SSK (submarine, hunter-killer, diesel-powered) *Santa Fe* and the *Santiago de Estero* and two German-built, electric-powered Type 209 SSCs (submarine, coastal) the *Salta* and the *Santa Cruz*. The *Santiago de Estero*

The damaged submarine Santa Fe in South Georgia.

and the *Santa Cruz* were unserviceable and the *Santa Fe* was lost at sea after being damaged at South Georgia. The SSCs were not designed for prolonged missions outside coastal waters. However, in time of war and in skilled and bold hands, they could be operated outside some of the limits set by the rule-book. They were particularly dangerous, being small and very quiet running. Each carried fourteen wire-guided torpedoes, and could stay at sea for 55 days. They were relatively easily refuelled, even in a FOB; their fuel cells

A battery change on a Type 209 SSC submarine.

- large batteries - could be replaced alongside from an improvised mother ship in a calm inlet.

Any Argentinian submarine would, however, be vulnerable to British counter-measures, honed to perfection in NATO exercises in the North Atlantic and Mediterranean.

On the other hand the CANA and the PNA were experienced in short range maritime patrols using small converted civil aircraft. These were to be especially useful for searching the shallow waters around the islands for submarines, fast assault craft and helicopters carrying raiding parties. The Argentinians had a healthy respect for, and knew a lot about, the SAS, SBS and Royal Marine Commandos.

All of those factors reinforced Argentinian interest in outlying islands with airfields and hills for radar and OPs. The Argentinians therefore decided to establish a strong presence on a northern island as a pre-emptive move. It was decided to deploy a CANA SRMPA flight, protected by an *Infanteria* unit, to somewhere on West Falkland. This force could conduct inshore reconnaissance patrols to locate any attempt by the British to land patrols or seize an island. The flight consisted of four Beechcraft T34C TurboMentors from the 4th Attack Squadron, and formed part of the *Grupo Aereo Insular* (GAI or Island Air Group), based at BAN Rio Grande, Tierra Del Fuego. The GAI was an ad-hoc formation comprising all CANA units and detachments deployed to the Falklands.

The Mentors were American-built two-seat armed trainers. They were flown by experienced aircrew and serviced by groundcrew used to operating on remote, primitive airstrips. Mentors could carry sufficient fuel for 750+ miles of low-level flight, giving a useful operating radius from any of the Falkland airstrips. They were fitted with wing racks for mounting rocket pods or machine-gun gondolas. The Argentinians used American LAU-6/68 reusable pods to launch 2.75-inch air-to-surface rockets; if fitted with the M247 shaped-charge anti-armour warhead they posed a serious threat to ships and surfaced submarines. The gondolas carried two 7.62mm guns and ammunition drums; deadly against helicopters, light craft, troops and soft-skin vehicles. Mentors were highly manoeuvrable, useful for avoiding Sea Harriers and engaging helicopters, and had a low infrared signature offering some protection from Sidewinder heat-seeking air-to-air missiles. (The pods and gondolas could be released in flight in case of an emergency.) However, the Mentors could only be operated during daylight as they were not fitted with night vision equipment and the GAI was not equipped with mobile night landing aids. Before the Mentors deployed, the radar 'shadow' was covered by Neptunes, operating as basic but efficient AWACs until they were eventually withdrawn as unserviceable.

To provide a ground attack capability against a British amphibious landing force, the FAA formed an ad-hoc unit, the *Escuadron Movil Pucara Malvinas*. It consisted of three flights of IA-58 *Pucara* light COIN (Counter-Insurgency) attack aircraft. The Pucaras – the name is derived from the ancient Amerindian fortresses found in the Andes - were designed for low altitude operations against lightly-armed insurgent groups and their hide-outs, so were fast, highly manoeuvrable and lightly armoured to survive small-arms fire. They were ideal aircraft for harassing amphibious landing operations and troops advancing across hilly country. Pucaras are fitted with four 7.62mm machine guns, two each side of the cockpit, and can also carry two 20mm cannon under the nose. Bombs, rockets pods, napalm or fuel tanks could be carried on three hard-points; one under the fuselage and below each wing. Pucaras deployed to the Falklands carried hard-points fitted with triple-ejection racks, allowing three bombs to be carried rather than one on the basic mounting. Pucaras are easy to service as they were designed for field operations: the low mounted wings enabling mechanics standing on the ground to check and adjust the engines. The aircraft could also be refuelled from hand-pumped petrol drums. Their main drawback, like the Mentors, was lack of night flying and attack equipment. Also, but not quite so important for what was seen as a short campaign, the airframes and engines had not been treated with anti-corrosion paint, essential for prolonged operations in a maritime environment. Another drawback was the aircrew's limited experience of maritime operations, apart from the long initial delivery flight to Stanley. Therefore, for inshore missions the Pucara aircrew would depend on CANA pilots in Mentors operating as pathfinders and Forward Air Controllers, once the issue of inter-operability of radios and radio procedures had been resolved; the CANA and FAA were rivals for funds and favours, and rarely if ever worked together.

On 13 April, the day the aerial survey was completed, CANA HQ confirmed the

The Pucara in flight showing two of its four 7.62mm machine guns. It could also carry two 20mm cannons under the nose.

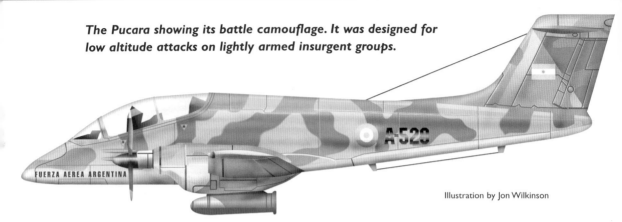

The Pucara showing its battle camouflage. It was designed for low altitude attacks on lightly armed insurgent groups.

Illustration by Jon Wilkinson

formation of the *Apoyo Aereo Cercano* [Inshore Air Support Unit] for SRMP/anti-shipping/anti-helicopter operations around the Malvinas. It would be equipped with two flying units and one of Marines for local protection. The anti-shipping role would be carried out by a flight of Italian-built Aeromacchi MB339 armed jet trainers based at Stanley. The SRMP Mentor flight was to be commanded by Lieutenant Jose Perrier and manned by air and ground crew from the *Escuala de Aviacion Naval* at BAN Punto Indio near Buenos Aires. The other pilots were Lieutenants Miguel Uberti, Marcelo Batllori and Luis Vidal. Like Pereyra Dozo they too were Qualified Flying Instructors and had flown SRMP missions in Patagonia and Tierra del Fuego.

The following day, 14 April, the commander of the GAI, Captain Alberto Olcese, initiated a survey of island airstrips in a commandeered FIGAS Islander plane. As a gesture of reconciliation, or to demonstrate that the new civil administration had returned things to normal, the mail and passenger service was reinstated. However, none of the three FIGAS pilots were available; one had a broken wrist but, like the others, would not fly under Argentinian command, so Captain Anselmi, as noted, took over the service and flew most flights until British air operations rendered such sorties too dangerous to continue.

That same day the FAA created BAM Condor, in other words the existing FIGAS airfield serving the twin settlements of Goose Green and Darwin. The original intention was for Condor to act as a FOB for Stanley. It would house FAA Pucaras, CANA Aeromacchis and Mentors and, at times, a PNA Puma helicopter in addition to maintenance and supply/service units, an AAA defence squadron, some FAA air observation posts and an Army defence force with infantry and light artillery units. On 21 April, after a few days of jostling with FAA Pucaras, *Ejercito*, PNA, FAA and CANA helicopters for the limited space and facilities at Goose Green, the then-senior *Armada* officer in the CCM at Port Stanley, Captain (Marine) Juan Moeremons, decided to seek an alternative FOB. As noted previously, the north coast of West Falkland was the obvious choice. That meant using either Carcass, Keppel or Pebble Islands. Examination of the results of the S2 Tracker survey led to Carcass being dismissed as too small, too remote and lacking in resources. Keppel

Island was too far from the open sea, lacked a harbour, flat ground and an abundant supply of freshwater (information found in Falklands government offices). Also, Keppel Island was too far across trackless country from Port Howard, the 'capital' of West Falkland, soon to be occupied by a strong garrison. That left Pebble Island.

That day, 24 April, the decision to station the Mentor flight on Pebble was formally endorsed and the aircraft arrived at Stanley later that day.

Argentinian naval bases are traditionally guarded by Marines and, in view of the British threat, the *Armada* ordered the Corps to provide additional protection for naval bases associated with Operation ROSARIO. The guard force was drawn from the 3rd 'Admiral Eleazar Videla' Marine Infantry Battalion, which in early 1982 had been deployed to Tierra del Fuego as part of the supporting element for ROSARIO. The ommanding officer, Lieutenant Colonel Raul Noziglia, instituted an intense training regimen in case the unit was required for operations. At that time the battalion consisted of a Command and

Infanteria de Marina.

Logistical Support Company and two Rifle ('*Tiradores*') Companies, G (officially 'Golf', but Garra to the Marines), and H (ditto Hotel/*Hacha*). As a peacetime expediency the third Rifle Company, I-(India), was in suspended animation. Each Rifle Company had a HQ Platoon and three Rifle and one Heavy Weapons Sections, but, temporarily, each Section had only two rifle groups instead of three. (Marine sections would be platoons in other nation's forces; each had a two-man HQ and three Rifle Groups, each of thirteen men.)

For its new role the battalion was reinforced with a section each of 107mm Heavy

Intanteria *75mm Recoilless Rifle. Note the firer positioned at the side to avoid the back blast.*

Mortars, 105mm Recoilless Rifles and Mamba wire-guided anti-tank missiles from other Marine units.[1] The 1st Marine Brigade supplied sufficient rifle groups to bring each section up to war establishment. (They were eventually allocated to G Company for use on the mainland.)

As the Company was to conduct independent operations it was to be further reinforced by a HQ Platoon with medical and communications personnel, and a section of 12.7mm Heavy Machine Guns. Further additions included two 81mm, mortars, and three 60mm, mortars. The latter were to illuminate targets for an Anti-tank Group equipped with three, 3.5inch Rocket Launchers.[2] The promised 105mm Recoilless Rifles were replaced with the 75mm version as they were smaller, lighter and fitted into most helicopters. The final Order of Battle for the 144-strong Company Group included three 28-man Squads, a Heavy Weapons Section with three machine gun groups and one each of mortars and rocket launchers. The HQ Platoon included the Company 2i/c. a Medical Officer and medical, communications, and the Heavy Weapons Section. The normal allocation of communications equipment was also increased to include PRC-377 and PRC-77 radios, batteries, battery chargers, a small mobile Kawasaki generator, petrol cans, 7 km of telephone cable, TP6 telephones and a ten-line ABM-1031 field telephone exchange. All combat personnel were to be issued with night vision equipment and batteries.

H Company had been selected to guard naval facilities on the Malvinas, specifically an unnamed naval air station; the FAA and CANA knew about the SAS and the SBS and their exploits against airfields in North Africa and the Eastern Mediterranean in the Second World War. They had good reason to prepare a strong defence force for, as suspected, the advancing Task Group included a strong contingent of Special Forces.

After a short delay, the Company flew into Stanley on 25 April, ready for anything.

FALKLANDS
PEBBLE ISLAND

DEFENCE

While H Company was moving across from the mainland, their combat engineer colleagues on Pebble were already hard at work. Their first task was to requisition the nearest settlement building to the airfield, a hut by the Marble Shanty track, as Field Defence Control Centre (FDCC). The next task was to rig the main pier with demolition charges in case there was an attempted enemy landing. This task was organised by Master Corporal Jorge Yeracci, and involved the preparation and emplacement of 37kg of TNT and PE, connected to the FDCC by 200 yard electric and pyrotechnic detonating cords. While that work was underway Master Corporal Osvaldo Lujan, assisted by Corporal Maguna, marked-out the location of three sets of demolition charges across the 310/130 airstrip. They also marked out and dug-back the turf from a shallow trench for the detonating cords, running back to the FDCC. Other engineers started to erect barbed wire fences around the settlement buildings selected for accommodation or stores. The residents observed this activity from behind their curtains with increasing anxiety.

By evening H Company had assembled on Stanley airfield, complete with two days worth of C Rations, and of ammunition at combat levels. Lieutenant Marega travelled into Stanley and reported to the *Armada* Section of the CCM HQ where he was briefed about Pebble Island by Sergeant Basualdo and provided with one of the precious photocopied maps. In the meantime the company was taken into Stanley by truck and installed for the night in the Drill Hall of the temporarily inactive Falklands Islands Defence Force. This had been arranged by Midshipman Orlando Sabbattini, a resourceful Marine Commando subaltern of the *Infanteria's Servicio para Apoyo de Combat*, (SPAC - Combat Support Service), detachment in Stanley. The Drill Hall provided rather basic and restricted accommodation but was infinitely preferable to sleeping in the open at the airport.

After an uncomfortable night and ablutions in the open air, a senior Marine officer arrived with bitter news; H Company was to be broken up. The decision had been taken the previous evening on the basis of greater need elsewhere than on Borbon. Only Lieutenant Marega and an attenuated force of 74 all ranks to be known as *Equipo Marega*, would deploy to Pebble and be reinforced as circumstances allowed. The *Equipo* consisted of a small HQ team, one Rifle and two Heavy Weapons Sections, one with four 75mm recoilless rifles, the other with two 7.62mm MAG General Purpose Machine Guns (GPMGs) equipped for the Sustained Fire role with heavy barrels, tripods and special sighting gear. The *Equipo*, apart from some of the Heavy Weapon crewmen, returned to the airport by truck and were then flown to their new base by PNA Skyvan and an Army Puma.

The first flight took Lieutenant Marega, his second in command, Midshipman Daniel Montalvo, who also commanded the Rifle Section and some marines. It arrived at 0900hrs and was met by Lieutenant Marquardt, who took Lieutenant Marega to the Big House. There, Marega informed Griff Evans that the settlement was now a military base and therefore under martial law. The inhabitants were to remain within the settlement area unless authorised to leave to tend the sheep, refrain from hostile acts and provide help when required, otherwise life would go on as before. None of the islanders believed that for a minute.

The marines made their way to the shearing shed, acquired bed-spaces in its spartan interior and were briefed on the rude cooking and toilet facilities by one of the Combat Engineers. Acting on Lieutenant Marega's orders Midshipman Montalvo, as the *Equipo*'s Quartermaster 'requisitioned' the estate's tractor and two Land Rovers, in addition to one belonging to the Berntsen family.

The two Marine officers immediately established a simple guard system. This included four guard posts, two on the airfield, one in the settlement and another by the long pier. They were manned in twelve-hour shifts, 0600-1800-0600 hrs.

The engineers continued to build up the base's defences. These included, oddly, demolition charges on the decrepit and little used small pier. The charges were rigged by Corporals Calbo and Vega with 30kg TNT and 10kg PE, and connected to the FDCC by duplicate detonating cords. Other engineers completed the airstrip demolition sets, using beehive-charges to blow narrow shafts into the rocky soil. They then used parachute cord entwined with the electric detonating wire to lower waterproofed charges of PE into the holes. These were then filled with soil and tamped and the detonating wires buried in trenches leading to the FDCC and partially attached to the detonating sets. Meanwhile work continued on erecting barbed wire fences between various buildings and the beach.

Around midday two Mentors arrived, flown by Lieutenants Pereyra and Uberti. They made some trial circuits and touch-and-go landings, followed by an aerial reconnaissance of the island. They then landed and made contact with Lieutenant Marquardt before returning to Stanley.

The following day, 27 April, those marines not on guard worked under Midshipman Montalvo to try to improve the shearing shed and the other requisitioned buildings for occupation by the garrison. The demolition works were completed and checked by Lieutenant Marquardt at 1000hrs. Thereafter some

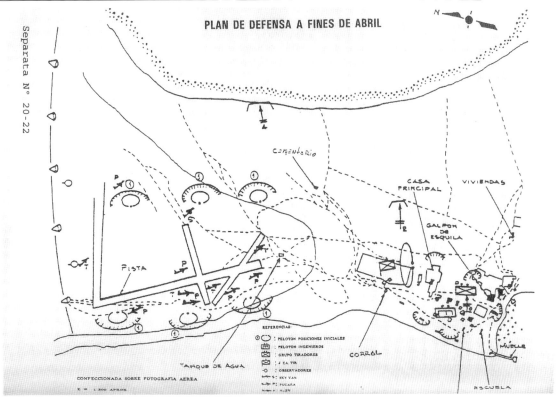

Lieutenant Marega's defence plan.

marines used the requisitioned tractor and a trailer to move defence stores to the upper (First Mountain) end of the airfield, where four engineers started to erect basic barbed wire barriers along the edge of the airfield, incorporating the existing fence. Others, directed by Lieutenant Marega, started to lay–out and spit-lock (remove the turf) trenches, ammunition bunkers and heavy-weapons positions covering the airfield and the approaches from Elephant Bay. Many of these were clustered at the west end of the main airstrip, at the highest point of the airfield and along the top of a low cliff. The sites covering the beach consisted of one large emplacement in the Sand Hills for all four 75mm recoilless rifles, and, further back towards the settlement, another emplacement for two 7.62 mm GMPGs in a sustained fire role.

During the late morning another Skyvan sortie brought more marines and supplies. A wireless message was received from the CCM in Stanley announcing that Lieutenant Pereyra had been appointed as *Jefe Escuadrilla y Estacion Aeronaval Bahia Elefante*; with Second Lieutenant (Aircraft Engineer) Livio Castro as 2i/c. Both arrived later that day in a Mentor.

Next day a Skyvan delivered yet more marines and some CANA communications and Air Traffic Control personnel. After being allocated living space in a requisitioned building the CANA men started to sort out their stores. They also set up a makeshift radio station in the new school, which had been appropriated by Lieutenant Pereyra as an Officer's Mess and Base HQ. It was provided with an extra-

43

Members of the Buzos Tacticos at Stanley after ROSARIO.

Buzos Tacticos qualification badge.

thick barbed wire fence with one entrance facing the settlement. Marega and Montalvo and their NCOs were convinced any attack would be delivered by the SBS, similar in many ways to the *Armada*'s highly trained Special Forces, the *Buzos Tacticos* with whom the *Infanteria* trained, or had provided 'enemy' for during exercises.[1] The School Hall was converted into a combined Air Traffic Control and Combat Operations Centre, the other rooms were used as sleeping quarters, dining and ante-rooms.

At 0937hrs the second two Mentors flew into Stanley from the mainland and after refuelling, continued on to *Borbon*, arriving at 1330hrs. After an initial briefing on the airfield by Lieutenant Pereyra and a look around the airfield and settlement, the pilots moved into their accommodation in the School.

The four Mentors were reportedly parked at pre-arranged dispersal sites along the redundant airstrips, initially marshalled by Lieutenants Pereyra and Uberti in the absence of groundcrew. The pattern of the parking slots appeared to be designed to place the aircraft outside the dispersal pattern of airfield attack weapon known to be used by the British.

CLUSTER BOMBS

Both the RAF and FAA used the Hunting Engineering BL755 cluster bomb in the Falklands. Each was loaded with 147 parachute-retarded bomblets, either the No.1 General Purpose or the No.2 anti-armour version. When dispersed from the bomb casing the bomblets covered an area of some 150 x 100 metres depending on altitude. Most are designed to explode on impact causing a combined anti-armour and anti-personnel effect, the latter blasting 2000 splinters for 100 metres from the point of detonation. Others have a delayed-action fuse to catch bomb disposal teams clearing the area.

Both Harrier types could carry one BL755 under each wing.

BL 755 dispensing bomblets and below one of the BL 755 bomblets.

Further Skyvan flights delivered more marines and equipment, and later in the day the MV *Forrest* arrived at the pier. As her radar was out of commission, (sabotage being suspected), she was escorted by the PIM patrol ship, GC82 *Islas Malvinas*. Her commander, First Officer Jorge Carrega, assisted by *Armada* Transport Service personnel, closely supervised *Forrest*'s usual crew. The cargo included some small trailers loaded with the marines' support weapons, various types of ammunition including 520 rounds for the recoilless rifles, barbed wire, drums of JP-1 aviation fuel, hand-pumps and fresh food for 30 days. There were also some supplies for the Officer's Mess, later described as, 'luxurious cheeses'.

The balance of the marines arrived the following day, 29 April, allowing the *Equipo* to be reported to the CCM as 'Combat Ready'. Another Skyvan flight delivered fourteen CANA groundcrew and five more Mentor pilots, who helped man the air traffic control centre during daylight hours in case of an emergency landing by a non-resident aircraft, or indeed any other incident. That allowed Lieutenant Pereyra to declare the *Escuadrilla* as 'Operational'.

The NCOs used a large house - which they described as 'the Infirmary', but which was just an empty house to the islanders - as a Mess. Staff Sergeant Carlos Ardaist, nominally i/c Recoilless Rifle Section, proceeded to act as a remarkably able cook.

The engineers finished marking-out six squad positions, two machine gun bunkers and the recoilless rifle emplacements to hold all four pieces, and started to excavate them. Lack of wood made provision of turf and soil overhead cover almost impossible; a few sheets of old corrugated iron had to suffice until more supplies were delivered from Stanley or the mainland. Despite a pasture-like appearance the ground proved to be rocky, requiring much use of explosives and hard work with pick axe and shovels. The promised reinforcements would complete the work – if and when they arrived. Barbed-wire entanglements were erected and a number of trenches dug.

The Marines used the Fire Trailer Hut as a comfortless Airfield Guard Room, but did not interfere with the appliance. Neither did the groundcrew attempt to test it: an unusual omission for staff of an operational airfield.

Throughout that day the CANA pilots had been conducting local area familiarisation and armed reconnaissance flights along the coast of West Falkland. In the afternoon one flight, consisting of the three fully serviceable Mentors, was diverted to intercept a live contact. At 1545hrs the CCM in Stanley plotted a possible helicopter landing at Berkeley Sound, north of the capital. The Mentors were ordered to intercept what Lieutenants Pereyra, Manzella and Uberti identified as a C4 Sea King. The Mentors were in turn plotted by a British ship, despite their small radar image (magnified by the spinning propeller blades) and the local British Combat Air Patrol (CAP) consisting of two Sea Harriers was alerted. One of them, flown by Lieutenant Commander 'Sharkey' Ward of 801 Squadron, made a single firing pass at the Mentor flight. A 30mm cannon round pierced the rear canopy of Pereya's Mentor. Fortunately he was not carrying an observer.

The Mentor flight scattered, releasing their machine-gun gondolas to increase speed and manoeuvrability and sought cover in the clouds. But the cat was out of the bag – the British realised there were enemy aircraft operating off the north coast

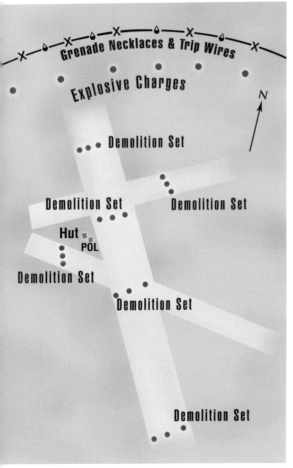

Grenade Necklaces & Trip Wires

Explosive Charges

N

Demolition Set

Demolition Set   Demolition Set

Hut
POL

Demolition Set

Demolition Set

Demolition Set

Booby-traps, explosive charges and airstrip demolitions as drawn from memory by Esteban, March 2006.

of West Falkland, implying a FOB to cover the sea area within the radar-shadow and the intended landing site at San Carlos Water. Such a base would be a serious threat so all efforts would be made to confirm that aircraft were indeed based on Pebble Island; just the task for Special Forces.

At 0930hrs on 30 April a Skyvan brought Captain (Marine) Craveri for a meeting with Lieutenants Pereyra, Marega and Marquardt to discuss their defence plans. The result was that the garrison was reinforced by a second Midshipman (Cesar Mazza), a second rifle section, a communications group of two NCOs and six marines with a second medical orderly. It was further agreed that as the main defence works had been completed some of the engineers could be released for urgent work on East Falkland; four left later that day, but Lieutenant Marquardt stayed until 4 May.

The Lieutenant's delayed departure was to ensure that an elaborate array of command-detonated anti-personnel devices was completed and made watertight as the weather had now broken.

1. A 'V' shaped set of 70 charges in the vicinity of Elephant Beach, each containing 200gms of explosive.

2. Grenade 'necklaces' triggered by trip-wires along the north & south edges of the airfield.

3. Six large (30kgs) explosive charges placed at intervals along the north side of the airfield. The two strings, and each of the charges, were controlled from the DFCC. These measures were in addition to the airstrip and pier demolition charges.

Later Lieutenants Pereyra and Vidal conducted a two-plane, armed reconnaissance of the remote Jason Islands, west of Pebble Island; nothing of military interest was noticed. However, while taxi-ing back to their parking spaces the nose-wheel strut of Lieutenant Pereyra's Mentor was damaged when it encountered a pot-hole in the airstrip, mistaken for a puddle. The damage could not be repaired immediately, but the aircraft was deemed flyable, and so not struck-off strength.

During the day, two *Ejercito* Augusta A-109 helicopters arrived at the airfield. They brought the 2nd Section, 601 Commando Company, re-activated in January 1982 specifically for Operation ROSARIO. By late April this unit, and the newly raised 602 Company, were being used to hunt for British Special Forces patrols and OPs across the entire Falkland group. That day the 2nd Section was searching the north coast of West Falkland, including Pebble and Westpoint Islands. They found nothing on Pebble Island but a partly deflated large red meteorological balloon. It was destroyed with hand grenades in case it was a weapon of some sort.

The marine reinforcements arrived by Skyvan at 1800hrs, bringing the number of personnel on *Borbon* to 114 all ranks.

The three *Infanteria* officers, who reportedly worked as a very close-knit, if nervous team, started to prepare an emergency scheme. It was called, bluntly, *Plan de Repliegue*, 'Retreat Plan', and covered both evasion from capture and escape from the island, in the event of a major attack. The plan involved the use of a large rubber boat fitted with an outboard motor belonging to one of the settlement families and a combat engineer Gemini. The former could carry twenty, the latter seven, armed and equipped soldiers. They were deflated and taken by Land Rover and tractor/trailer combination to Ship Harbour, at the eastern end of the island, re-inflated and tested and concealed next to a stream, well above high water mark. (During one of these trips the Berntsen's Land Rover became bogged down.) In the event of an emergency evacuation any troops gaining the opposite shore were to head east to find a telephone line linking Port Howard with White Rock House, turn left and follow it south to the safety of the former, by then HQ of a large garrison.

The islanders settled into a restricted routine. They, too, were nervous, and among other things prepared simple bunkers among the stone foundations under the floorboards of their houses. Few had seen so many people in one place for an extended period and did not enjoy the experience, although the garrison was more surly rather than antagonistic.

That day the British Task Groups were recorded as being 100 miles north of the Falklands, and all Argentinian bases were warned that an attack or landing could be expected in the near future.

On May Day Stanley airfield was attacked at 0440hrs and some damage done to aircraft and installations. As a result the CCM ordered the dispersal of as many resident aircraft as possible, mainly to Goose Green/Darwin, by then renamed BAM Condor. However, later that day a combined Harrier attack on that base destroyed three out of fourteen Pucaras, killing a pilot and nine groundcrew. A recce mission of two Pucaras, led by Captain Roberto Vila flying in A-502, was immediately sent to reconnoitre the *Borbon* and Port Howard airstrips for use as a dispersal area. The

GR3 HAWKER HARRIER

The Hawker Harrier proved to be a formidable enemy during the Falklands campaign. It was agile and wasn't reliant on airstrips and runways.

XV740

Illustration by Jon Wilkinson

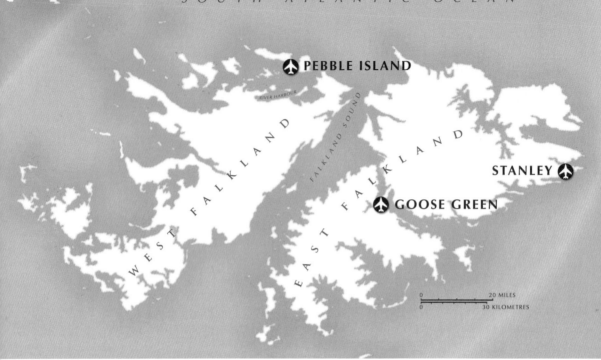

PEBBLE ISLAND

RIVER HARBOUR

WEST FALKLAND

FALKLAND SOUND

EAST FALKLAND

STANLEY

GOOSE GREEN

```
0        20 MILES
0        30 KILOMETRES
```

ARGENTINE AIRBASES ON THE FALKLANDS.

latter was rejected after a quick fly-by. After a survey of *Borbon*'s facilities and a long discussion with the naval pilots and some laborious refuelling, the Pucaras departed at 1230hrs, satisfied that a dispersal site had been located. That brought the total to three Argentinian air bases on the Falklands.

During the afternoon six Pucaras arrived from Goose Green. However, during its landing aircraft A-523 slid off the airstrip and became bogged down. As there was no equipment or vehicle on the island capable of moving it from the soft earth it was struck-off charge and remained at the side of the airstrip at a drunken angle.

The Harrier/Mentor incident of 29 April had alerted the British to an air presence on West Falkland without them locating the base. A few days later, on 4 May, there was a clue. British radar operators plotted intense air activity north of Stanley. Despite frozen grass strips at *Borbon*, which grounded the Pucaras, the Mentors were active. They were part of Operation Margarita, a combined arms sweep of Long Island to destroy possible British Special Forces bases. The troops included the *Gendarmeria Nacional's* Scorpion Squadron, raised, like the Commando Companies, for Operation *ROSARIO*. It was manned by fit, tough and aggressive personnel, some of whom had recent

Gendarmeria Nacional *Scorpion* Squadron after arriving at Stanley Airport.

KEPPEL ISLAND

PEBBLE ISLAND

PEBBLE

TAMAR PASS

FOUL BAY

WHITE ROCK BAY

HILL COVE

PORT SAN CARLOS

SAN CARLOS ESTATE

FALKLAND SOUND

WEST FALKLAND

PORT HOWARD

EAST FALKLAND

SEA HARRIER RADAR 'HIT', 7 MAY 1982.

experience of offensive patrols against insurgents. The British SAS, SBS and the Mountain and Arctic Warfare Cadre (MAWC) patrols were no longer to operate with impunity. The sweep was conducted by helicopter-mounted gendarmes, commandos and marines, intent on following-up sightings made from Mentors flying out of *Borbon*; nothing unusual was discovered, but the Royal navy radar plotters assessed that the aircraft came from Pebble Island.

A further clue reportedly came on 7 May, with the chance interception of a brief radar emission. A Sea Harrier pilot flying north of East Falkland heard a squawk in his earphones as the tail-mounted Radar Warning Receiver recorded a brief 'hit'. The receiver was not fitted with a library of radar signatures, so only the bearing, approximate height of the emitter, and type of emission was identified, not the source. Analysis of the information seemed to place the emitter on either Middle Mountain or Keppel Island's Cove Hill. That had serious implications for British operations in Falkland Sound, by then the preferred site for the Amphibious Operations Area. There was widespread concern, both in London and afloat, regarding an apparent Argentinian air threat to the Task Groups as the inadequacy of their anti-air defences were probably well-known to the Argentinians. Naval doctrine requires air (and maritime) superiority, if not supremacy, if an amphibious operation is to succeed. The Royal Navy had enjoyed air, surface and sub-surface supremacy for all of its modern landings, from Gallipoli to Suez, but in early May 1982 it had, at best, air parity.

The immediate requirement was to find out exactly what, if anything, was on, or afloat near Pebble Island in order to assess the threat. The subsequent search

RAF Nimrod R1.

involved three main thrusts. The first was heightened electronic surveillance using all assets, national or foreign, available to the British intelligence community. The means of collection included ships, shore-based stations and aircraft such as RAF Nimrod R1 ELINT aircraft of 53 Squadron. One operated from Ascension Island, and on 8 May, another, courtesy of Chile, flew a mission from San Felix Island, a Chilean base and airfield set on the Islas de los Desventurados, far out in the South Pacific. It was spotted overhead, but not identified, by *Infanteria* and CANA personnel on Pebble Island.

The second source was visual and photographic reconnaissance by Sea Harriers which carried sideways-looking nose cameras. The third source was much more personal and involved 'eye ball' reconnaissance of the base by Special Forces.

FALKLANDS
PEBBLE ISLAND

SPECIAL FORCES

The Operation **CORPORATE** Task Force included Special Forces from all three services with the vast majority of the personnel afloat with one or other of the Task Groups. The Army supplied elements of the Special Air Service Regiment, and the Royal Marines part of the Special Boat Squadron.[1] In 1982 the difference between them was, roughly, that the **SBS** operated below the top of the inter-tidal zone and was manned by Marines while the **SAS** operated above it and had for some years recruited from all three services. Also available was the Medium-Range Reconnaissance Patrol Team manned by Mountain Leaders from the RM Mountain and Arctic Warfare Cadre[2] (MAWC) commanded by Captain Rod Boswell RM, and a very small RAF component.[3] All of these were supported by Fleet Air Arm helicopter aircrew well-versed in special forces tasks and, at times, by 1st Raiding Squadron, RM, operating fast assault craft and commanded by Captain Chris Baxter, RM.

SAS beret badge.

SBS beret badge (introduced 2004).

These detachments formed the largest operational concentration of British Special Forces since 1945 but even then were insufficient: more could have been used in the early stages of the campaign. As a result they were briefly augmented for a time by teams from D (Patrols) Company, 3rd Battalion Parachute Regiment. Later, after the fatal helicopter crash of 19 May, personnel from B Squadron 22 SAS arrived by parachute.

The SBS group was allocated to the Commander, Amphibious Warfare Task Group (Commodore Clapp) to conduct specific Advance Force Operations, mainly landing site and seaway reconnaissance. The SAS and the MAWC were allocated to the Commander, Landing Force (Brigadier Julian

Mountain Leader Grade I qualification badge.

Thompson) with a variety of pre-and post landing, land reconnaissance missions and raids as required. The three Special Forces commanders were based on HMS *Fearless*, close to Brigadier Thompson's HQ, which was in close contact with that of Commodore Clapp. The SAS and MACW detachments were tasked by the Special Forces Liaison Officer, Colonel Richard Preston RM, although both the COs were consulted about general matters by Admiral Woodward, Commodore Clapp and Brigadier Thomspon.

The SBS detachment consisted of 2, 3 and 6 Sections and a small HQ, commanded by Major Jonathan Thomson, the first non-SBS officer to command the Squadron. A recce, such as that of Pebble Island would normally have been an SBS task but all three Sections were involved in 'FOB watching' and beach surveys.[4] That left the Landing Force's dedicated Special Forces units; but as the MAWC was preparing to deploy onto East Falkland there was only the SAS left to call upon.

The SAS detachment consisted of two elements, one in the UK and one afloat. Both were manned by the all-regular 22 SAS; the two Territorial Army units - 21 and 23 SAS Regiments - were not mobilised. The UK element was headed by the Director SAS Group, Brigadier Peter de la Billiere, supported by a Special Operations Group Cell in the Army section of the Operation CORPORATE centre in the Ministry of Defence.

The detachment afloat was led by Lieutenant Colonel Michael Rose, commanding 22 SAS. His team consisted of a Tactical HQ and men from D, G and later, B Squadrons. Rose's Tactical HQ, which occupied Portakabins lashed to the foredeck of HMS *Fearless*, included personnel from 16 (SAS) Squadron Royal Signals and 603 Tactical Air Control Party, one of the very few RAF Special Forces units. (Aircraft, aircrew and mission planning staff of the Special Duties flight of 47 Squadron RAF were also involved in Operation CORPORATE).

SAS SQUADRONS

In 1982 22 SAS had four Sabre squadrons, A, B, D and G*.

Squadrons were commanded by a Major, with a small HQ including a Squadron Sergeant Major and a Squadron Quartermaster Sergeant, plus a clerk, a storeman, and an armourer. Squadrons consisted of four Troops, each commanded by a Captain, with a Staff Sergeant as 2i/c and both also led one of their Troop's four, 4-man patrols. Troops were roughly numbered consecutively throughout the regiment in order of raising the squadrons, hence 1-4 for A Squadron and the seemingly otherwise illogical 16-19 for D Squadron.

Of the four Troops in a Squadron, Air Troop go to war by helicopter, aircraft and parachutes (and, very occasionally, balloons), Boat Troop use wetsuits, canoes and small craft. Mobility Troop operate on motorbikes and in light vehicles while Mountain Troop go to war the hard way; using toes, fingers, ropes, pitons, skis and sledges.

*The omission of 'C' perpetuates the memory of the Rhodesian-manned Squadron raised for 22 SAS in Malaya in the early 1950s.

Carcass Island, possible site of Argentinian FOB. Galen R Frysinger

Lieutenant Colonel Rose had attended the initial debriefing of NP 8901, the Falklands garrison captured during the Argentinian invasion and then repatriated, shortly after their arrival at RAF Brize Norton. The process was greatly assisted by the presence of Major Ewen Southby-Tailyour, RM, who had commanded NP8901 during 1978-79. He was an authority on the Falklands terrain, coastline and their defence, including possible landing sites for amphibious and SF operations, bases and OPs. Planning for a reconnaissance of Pebble, and other locations including Carcass and Keppel Islands, had started in mid-April, in relation to a British FOB. Lieutenant Colonel Rose had given much thought to Special Forces operations and he and his staff continued to research the subject during the journey south, with frequent reference to Major Southby-Tailyour.

The problem was lack of troops and helicopters. G Squadron's eight patrols were committed to intelligence collection for Brigadier Thompson, leaving D Squadron for any Pebble Island operation. Commanded by Major Cedric Delves, D Squadron had already seen hard service in the South Atlantic, on South Georgia. There they had had a trying time, partly due to poor equipment, partly to over-confidence. The Squadron was then reassembling on *Hermes* and under the eye of the Squadron Sergeant Major Laurie Gallagher, familiarising themselves with equipment supplied by the US Special Forces Group, Fort Bragg, North Carolina. New items included SATCOM radios which allowed operators to communicate directly with London, Tactical HQ and other the patrols; the signals were undetectable by the *Ejercito*'s efficient *Seccion de Operaciones Electronicas 602* in Stanley. The helpful Americans also provided some useful weapons, complete with ammunition and instructions. They included M203 grenade launchers which fitted onto the SAS's M-16 rifles, and fired 40mm high explosive and smoke grenades out to 350 metres.

On 7 May D Squadron received a warning order for an imminent operation, task unspecified. However, only the equivalent of three full troops were available. Such was the urgent need for information and the scarcity of SBS sections, a patrol, thought to have been from Boat Troop, was watching for Argentinian minelaying in Falkland Sound. That meant only a depleted squadron was available for reconnaissance of Pebble Island, any rescue mission if anything went wrong, and a follow-up assault.

In the meantime, aboard HMS *Fearless*, Lieutenant Colonel Rose and his HQ team reviewed their options and refined their plans for a 'wet' insertion of a reconnaissance patrol onto Pebble Island.

A 'wet insertion' was usually by surface vessel, submarine, parachute or helicopter onto an offshore drop zone. There was no submarine to hand - HMS *Onyx* was on its way, and nuclear submarines keep well away from inshore waters. The launch could be from the radar-picket, at that time a frigate such HMS *Broadsword*, posted north of Pebble Island to give early warning of hostile inbound raids against the ships of the British fleet . The patrol could either land from rigid raider assault boats of 1st Raiding Squadron, the Troop's own Gemini-powered (and after South Georgia, suspect) boats or by Klepper canoes – scarcely considered due to the sea-state. A wet insertion meant using No 17 (Boat) Troop, commanded by Captain Timothy Burls of the Parachute Regiment.

The SAS team devised a plan and then consulted Major Southby-Tailyour, telling him only that they had been tasked with eliminating a radar thought to be on Middle Mountain. The SAS ideas did not coincide with his views, so in turn he sought the advice of Major Thomson, commanding the SBS Detachment. He in turn conferred with Captain Howard, his Operations Officer. Their view was that a landing could best be effected at Pebble Cove by night on a rising tide, following the line of a bank of floating kelp into the shore, then using the crest of the inbound swell for concealment. However, strengthening westerly gales and high seas (Sea State 7; High with 6-9 metre waves) quickly ruled out the use of small craft. The problems of South Georgia were fresh in everyone's minds - helicopter crews, mission planners, army and navy and especially the SAS men who had so nearly been swept away on a lengthy and unplanned visit to New Zealand! Any plan using a Gemini motor was thus rejected. That left canoes.

By 10 May intelligence had revealed that Pucaras and other aircraft were on Pebble Island. At a meeting on HMS *Hermes* to discuss the issue that day, Admiral Woodward stressed to Lieutenant Colonel Rose the urgency of removing this threat and any associated radar or other weapon systems which might harm his ships and aircraft. A Harrier cluster-bomb attack could not be certain of destroying all the enemy aircraft and airfield facilities, quite apart from the dreaded issue of possible 'collateral damage'. Any injury to British subjects and their property would be a public relations gift to the Argentinians. (That was to happen at Dunnose Head Farm, on the west coast of West Falkland when Tim Miller was injured during a Sea Harrier attack. He was injured by a cluster-bomb splinter and lost an eye but was able to join his brother Sam on Keppel Island. The Argentinians, as far as can be discerned, did not exploit this 'blue-on-blue' incident.) In response Lieutenant Colonel Rose stated that mounting an airfield raid on Pebble Island might require as much as three weeks preparation. It was something no SAS unit had undertaken since 1945, although the Regiment had, over many years, been used to test the defences of RAF airfields during Tactical Evaluations; rigorous tests of varying intensity designed to sharpen up all aspects of operational capability, not just defence. Added to which there was nothing to hand resembling the famed Lewes Bombs. These aircraft demolition charges had been devised in the autumn of 1941

German aircraft destroyed by the SAS during World War Two.

Taylor Library

Aircraft sabotage pioneers of World War Two, Jock Lewes and David Stirling.

at Kabrit, Egypt, by Lieutenant Jock Lewes, who, with David Stirling was the co-founder of SAS raiding techniques. Basically a fuse attached to 1lb of plastic explosive, heavy oil and thermite (aluminium and iron oxide powders, which, if combined, burned at 2500°C), Lewes Bombs were detonated by a time-pencil. The blast burned through an aircraft's aluminium skin to ignite residual fuel in wing or fuselage tanks. If anything like that was indeed available in 1982 none were to be found in the magazines of Her Majesty's Ship *Fearless*. Instead there were LAWs; Light Anti-armour Rockets, fired from disposable tubes.

Despite these caveats, Admiral Woodward was adamant. He indicated that the timetable for the landings, dictated in part by the imminent onset of winter, meant that all resources would be required to support the landings, scheduled for a date between 16 and 25 May. Therefore the raid would preferably have to be mounted on 13 May, to allow servicing on the 14th followed by intense use during final pre-landing cross-decking on 15 May.

Lieutenant Colonel Rose got to work on what someone named Operation PRELIM. He and Major Delves had already decided to insert a patrol that night, 10/11 May, deploying the men and their canoes into the sea north-east of Pebble Island from the duty radar picket. The possibility of radar on Middle Mountain precluded a covert landing on Pebble Island so it was decided to land a reconnaissance group of two-patrols, complete with four ready-assembled Kleppers, onto the northern shore of Port Purvis, an almost land-locked bay leading-off Pebble

KLEPPER CANOE

The Klepper canoe was used by reconnaissance groups of Boat Troop to make a covert landing on Pebble Island.

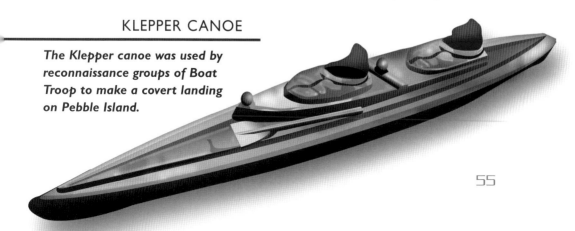

A Special Forces unit using a Klepper canoe.

Island Sound. The landing site would be out of sight of any observers on Pebble equipped with night vision equipment and lay within the radar shadow of low hills south west of White Rock House.

Eventually the weather and sea-state made an offshore Klepper insertion from a surface ship impossible; leaving only helicopters. However, these were in short supply. By 10 May there were only fourteen Sea King C4 (Commando) helicopters on *Hermes*, only four of which were fitted for use by night vision equipped aircrew practised in Special Forces missions. Three Sea Kings had already been lost, two on the unfortunate SAS mission on South Georgia and Commander Clapp was apprehensive about losing any more on Special Forces operations. However, there was no other method of getting a reconnaissance patrol into the vicinity of Pebble Island, so Admiral Woodward sanctioned the use of C4s, launched from *Hermes*; which, with two air-defence and anti-submarine escorts, would have to move westwards, twice, into dangerous waters

HELICOPTER INSERTION OF SPECIAL FORCES

By 1982 the Fleet Air Arm had long-since relinquished its propeller-driven COD-4 [Carrier On-board Delivery] Gannet aircraft, once considered for parachute delivery of SBS swimmer-canoeists.

Parachuting from helicopters may sound odd and indeed a helicopter slowing and then stopping for landing can easily be plotted by radar. C4 Sea Kings could, at a pinch, be used for parachute insertion of patrols. While the invasion force assembled at Ascension, personnel from 846 Squadron and an RAF parachute jump instructor, assisted by Royal Marine and Parachute Regiment jump instructors, tried parachuting from a C4. The technique worked, more or less, but was not used. If nothing else there were too few helicopters to devote one or more to parachuting. The technique was not deemed safe, the supply of suitable parachutes and other equipment was limited and would only have served to clutter the already bulging *Hermes*.

To avoid detection by radar on Pebble Island and near Stanley, a circuitous low-level route was necessary, hopping from one radar shadow to another, further complicated by the strong westerly winds. There was also the possibility that a patrolling Neptune or Tracker might detect the helicopter, even with their surface-search radars and, by simple plotting of back-bearings, identify the probable location of *Hermes* and her escorts. The Argentinian surveillance aircraft had been plotted flying racecourse orbits southwest of the Falklands and had been 'hunted' by HMS *Glasgow*, a Sea Dart-fitted destroyer, when operating south of Stanley.

Apart from radar detection there was the problem of getting *Hermes* and her escorts within flying range of Pebble, yet as far as possible from Argentinian airbases on the mainland. This required the ships to sail into the main air-threat axis in order to reduce the flight time and so increase the payload of the C4s, a bold but calculated risk. Admiral Woodward and Commodore Clapp were seriously concerned about sailing *Hermes* within range of Argentinian air sorties, concerns exacerbated by a submarine threat, with attacks possibly timed to coincide with air attacks.

ARGENTINIAN SUBMARINES

At the time of the Exocet attack on HMS *Sheffield*, several of the anti-submarine warfare screen's helicopters and surface ships gained sonar contacts near the Task Groups.[5] Many were prosecuted without obvious damage to submarines, although the local whale population is thought to have suffered. In fact only ARA *Salta* was active around the Falklands but her numerous attacks failed due to malfunctioning torpedoes, torpedo tubes and periscope gear.

The final plan involved launching the C4 from a point within the radar-shadow about 100 miles from West Falkland. It would then fly inland, north-west of Mount Rosalie and land the group at Port Purvis. After checking the area was clear of Argentinians the SAS would load the canoes and paddle out of the bay via Purvis Narrows, then, hugging the shore north of Purvis Point, follow the shore-line of Whale Bay and land in a secluded inlet at the foot of Deep Ferny Valley. They would then establish a lying up position (LUP) in that deep gully and, before dawn, establish an OP on either Round Hill or Foresight Hill. During the day observers would study the east end of Pebble Island and the airfield. According to their maps the settlement would be just out of sight behind Ram's Head ridge.

The following night the group would paddle across Whale Bay and Pebble Sound to land near Phillips Cove, on Pebble Island. They then had several tasks. One half-patrol was to check the immediate area for any signs of Argentinian defences or patrols, then find and establish an OP and an associated LUP to cover the cove. The other two men from the patrol were to reconnoitre Phillips Cove, selected from a map as being within the radar shadow of the Stanley and (hopefully) any Pebble radars and report its suitability as a helicopter landing zone. The other patrol was to reconnoitre the airfield and settlement area. That would include setting up OPs/LUPs and studying any defences, especially any air defence or fire-support weapon systems. If necessary two members of each patrol would conduct night time reconnaissance of any suspected threat to the Task Force, or indeed to an SAS raiding party, not determined accurately by observation. The airfield patrol was to plot routes (including obstructions) to and from the airstrip area from the intended landing zone and, at a point about 2,000 metres from the airfield, a base-plate

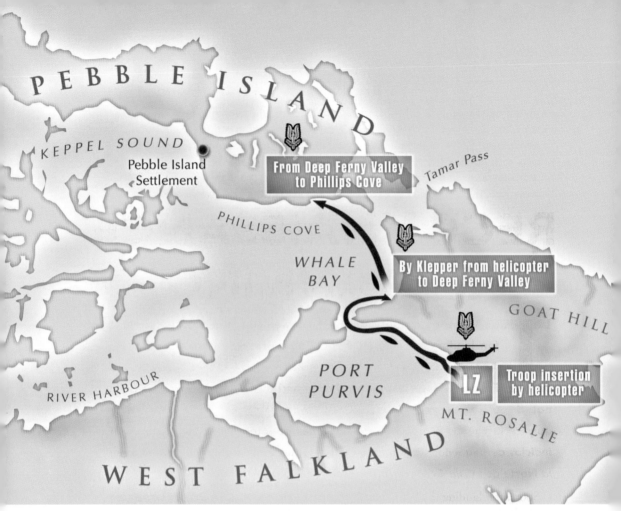

17 TROOP'S PLAN TO REACH PEBBLE ISLAND BY KLEPPER.

position for a 81mm mortar which would supplement or replace naval gunfire support.

The weather did not improve and on 10 May, as time was pressing, it was decided to land the recce group that night, with the remainder of Boat Troop on stand-by to reinforce, recover, or replace them. However, once *Hermes* and her escorts were approaching the fly-off point the weather was considered too bad to launch and recover helicopters, so the mission was postponed and the ships withdrew to safety. But in moving west their positions had been plotted by the Stanley radar crews and their turning point assessed. That information was reported by the CCM to all and sundry, including the Argentinian garrison on *Borbon*. Now, although the worst fears of the Argentinians on Pebble Island regarding a British landing had not exactly been confirmed they had certainly been heightened. The British, it seemed, had already been and taken a look at their front door.

RECONNAISSANCE & PLANNING

The following evening, 11 May, the weather was deemed suitable for landing - misty, with light rain offering poor visibility for Argentinian observers - and the abbreviated 17 Troop duly landed on West Falkland. The movement of ships and the inbound flight was again noted (possibly by one of the last Neptune flights), plotted at Stanley and duly reported by the CCM, *'Por informes de inteligencia, aumentaron los indicios de pequeños desembarcos y movimientos de comandos británicos en la Norte de la isla Gran Malvina.'*

Soon after landing the group encountered trouble. Heavy surf, exaggerated by the westerly winds and the incoming tide surging through the Narrows, made canoeing

WHALE BAY

DEEP FERNY VALLEY

WEST END

ROCK

LUP AREA

PURVIS POINT

ROUND HILL

MACKINTOSH'S RIDGE

MACKINTOSH'S PASS

PURVIS NARROWS

FERNY BANK

CROSS COUNTRY ROUTE TO DEEP FERNY VALLEY

PORT PURVIS

GARDEN HILL

LZ

impossible. There was nothing for it but to report to Tactical HQ, break down the Klepper canoes, pack them in their hold-alls and haul them, moving tactically, over Mackintosh's Ridge then down into Deep Ferny Valley to avoid any movement on the north-west face of Round Hill. The journey had to be made twice, because everyone was fully equipped and heavily armed and the bagged Kleppers weighed around 50 lbs each. It was an experience to be remembered, but not with affection.

The group established an LUP above the water's edge in the Valley, and spent the day – the weather being recorded by the assiduous FAA meteorological staff as 'changeable, with rain'- under what little cover could be found. Operation *PRELIM* was now one day behind schedule. During daylight it was not possible to find an OP from which to observe Pebble Island. Therefore the group posted sentries, kept as dry as possible on a Falkland morning in late autumn, and caught some sleep. After stand-to, at sunset and then again at stand-down, the upper slopes of the two hills were scouted, and an OP established on the barren slopes between the two hills.

At *Borbon* orders were received from the CANA HQ relieving Lieutenant Pereyra of command and posting him to a new task in Stanley.

That night the airfield guard reported a *Bengala verde*, a green flare, over Elephant Bay. The garrison sounded the General Alarm and went to Action Stations but nothing further happened. The source of this flare had not been identified during research for this book.

Throughout the following day, 13 May, the OP above Deep Ferny Valley was used to observe Pebble Island by telescope and binoculars and to record local air activity. That included an Argentinian Chinook using terrain-masking to hide from naval radar and Sea Dart missiles. The Chinook was carrying supplies to *Borbon*. Whilst outbound over West Falkland the helicopter's crew received a Red Alert from Stanley, warning them of Harriers in their vicinity. In the course of evasive manoeuvres the NCO Loadmaster was hit by shifting cargo and received internal injuries so the flight was aborted to get him to hospital. Another sortie was mounted and the Chinook delivered the much-needed supplies to *Borbon*. It also brought a

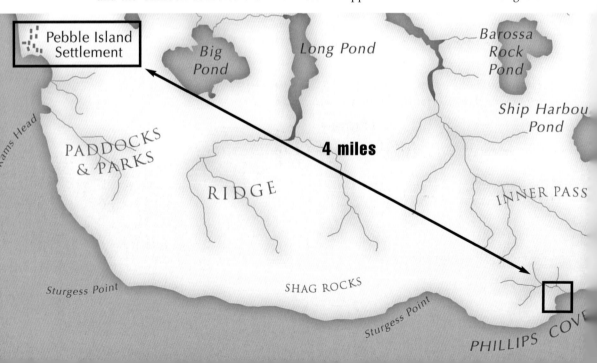

personal note from Midshipman Sabbattini for Lieutenant Marega, advising him that as the supply situation was becoming difficult the load included as much as could be spared over the official thirty days allocation for the reduced establishment.

That night, after a brief stand-to, the SAS group assembled the flexible-framed Kleppers, then loaded and launched them, ready for the crossing to Pebble Island.

Late on 13 May the canoes were paddled across Whale Bay, their crews endeavouring to avoid the tidal rip south of Inner Pass by crossing at slack water at midnight, to land near Phillips Cove, just over four miles from the settlement, at around 0400hrs.

SLACK WATER

This is a time or location when or where no appreciable current is flowing in a body of water. At sea, slack water usually occurs when the tide turns so can be calculated accurately for most locations from tide-tables.

HMS *Fearless*'s Navigating Officer, Lieutenant Commander John Prime, had been co-opted to act as Staff Navigation Officer. He supplied most of the slack water times for special forces and the main landing force operations. According to Ewen Southby-Tailyour's book, *Falkland Island Shores*, at the full or new moon, high water at Tamar Harbour is at 8.45; by adding 50 minutes for each day after that the high tide time can be calculated.

The patrols immediately set up all-round defence until satisfied there was no welcoming committee. They then started to check the area for signs of enemy activity - and immediately discovered that the area behind the beach was covered in a stretch of water not shown on their maps. This area had been tentatively identified as the helicopter landing zone for a raid as it was sheltered by low bluffs and approachable at low level in the radar shadow.

Right: A portion of the reconnaissance map which did not indicate the pond behind the beach.

Photograph of Phillips Cove showing the stretch of water (right) which was intended to be the helicopter LZ. Allan White

PHILLIPS COVE

61

The patrol continued to check the area. To the east of the landing point, on top of the bluff, there were recent vehicle tracks. (Made by requisitioned Land Rovers moving the rubber boats.) Two men stayed on guard on the bluffs while the Kleppers were unloaded, dismantled and concealed and the signaller sent a brief situation report. Captain Burls then led the group off to reconnoitre the settlement and airfield and the routes between them and the cove, leaving a small guard at the landing zone.

While moving forward cautiously, the patrols were not to know that the Argentinian garrison did not carry out roving patrols away from the airfield, day or night, the SAS attempted to keep in contact with the LUP by radio. Due to the flat terrain, however, and the proximity to each other, the only way contact could be established and maintained was to set up a relay station, manned by two men, on the highest point of the plateau, which, handily, was near the dell selected from the map for a possible mortar base-plate position. Captain Burls and the other troop members carried on, moving carefully just below the crest of each low ridge as the Argentinians were known, thanks to the US Marine Corps which had trained them, to be equipped with good night vision equipment.

The men skirted the settlement and moved through the edge of the Sand Hills to the north end of Elephant Beach, attempting to find a suitable site for an OP, preferably under cover, on the eastern flank of First Mountain. But daylight was fast approaching, so they had to lie flat near a stream running down into the sea. This site provided a limited view over the airfield and almost nothing of the settlement. All that could be seen in the dim light of dawn were one or two canvas-covered mounds, possibly oil drums or ammunition boxes and the outlines of some aircraft, including the distinctive profiles of Pucaras. This was enough to confirm that a threat existed on Pebble Island. Captain Burls relayed a brief message to Tactical HQ. It was a masterpiece of understatement: 'Eleven, repeat eleven, aircraft. Believed real [i.e. not dummies]. Squadron attack tonight. LS Phillips [Cove]. NFI . Send ETA.'

The observers continued to scrutinise the airfield. Due to the terrain they were unable to plot the positions of all the aircraft, and were, despite Captain Burls' message, unable to make an accurate count. They particularly watched for signs and sounds of troops 'standing-to' arms from at least 30 minutes before sunrise to anything up to one hour after; there was little to note. Not long after sunrise movement around the Fire Tender Hut seemed to indicate the presence of a night guard, and later there was some sort of changeover to a day watch. Shortly after that some groundcrew appeared, straggling up from the area of the settlement. They proceeded to remove the canvas shrouds from the aircraft radiator-inlets and cockpits and to carry out pre-flight checks. All that could be seen of defence works was some barbed wire around what appeared to be bunkers and trenches and in one case, fuel or oil drums under a tarpaulin, by a hut.

There was no sign of a radar set, control cabin and generator, either camouflaged or otherwise. Nor was there any sight or sound of a heavy generator, only the growling of a small one, maybe two, coming from the settlement, where breakfast time was approaching.

There were no signs of guns or missile launchers. However, the possibility of a

Roland wheeled TEL and its associated radar vehicle, or a trailer-mounted, visually guided Tigercat launcher and light anti-aircraft guns being concealed in the shearing shed could not be discounted. These could also be placed, camouflaged, alongside any building, ready to be moved into a firing position. There were no signs of gun positions or mortar pits, or of large, irregular shaped humps with camouflage netting stretched over thin, metal umbrella-like frames or strung between wooden props to conceal artillery pieces. The only vehicles noted during the day were a civilian Land Rover and a tractor, both pulling trailers and both manned by servicemen.

There was no sign of fuel bowsers or any airfield support vehicles such as a crane for changing engines, lifting bogged aircraft, or for assisting with wheel changes or undercarriage leg repairs; both prime SAS targets since North African days. Nor was there any evidence of a workshop trailer, tent or shack in the area.

There were a few signs of Argentinian field toilets, a necessity on an airfield and especially one containing a spring supplying drinking and cooking water to the ground and aircrew and of course the locals. FAA and CANA units rarely deployed for long periods onto airstrips, let alone into the field, without support facilities, not even the Pucara counter-insurgency squadrons. The motley detachment on Pebble Island therefore lacked such essentials as toilet buckets and canvas or hessian screens, metal or plastic bowls for washing hands or stands or chairs to support them. The few toilets in the school, shearing shed and workshop were well patronised (the garrison suffered from diarrhoea) as were extempore facilities such as 'hole and shovel' arrangements. But toilet paper was in rather short supply for the garrison so, as Raymond Evans tactfully put it, *'you had to watch where you walked ...Even the cowshed was used* [as a toilet] *after we refused to provide the troops with milk.* Note that the Argentinians did not attempt to force the issue, although in other respects some of them were light-fingered and *'pinched anything they could lay there hands on',* a habit found in any armed service, of any nation, sometimes referred to as 'liberating'.

The SAS men had been briefed on the aircraft, helicopters, radar and air defence systems they might encounter around the airstrips. The intelligence staff on *Fearless* had supplied Boat Troop with silhouettes and photographs from *Janes All The World's Aircraft,* and other sources. The observers studied two Pucaras parked, apparently at random, on the upper airfield. They were not covered with camouflage nets and were painted dusty brown and grey-green, ideal for the Argentinian pampas or the Chaco wilderness, but unlike the deeper greens and browns of Pebble Island's open ground. There were no signs of blast-walls of peat blocks, turf or rock.

The observers remained on watch until after sunset at 4:30 p.m. They were expecting to see the garrison 'standing to arms' from at least 30 minutes before and after sunset; nothing like that appeared to take place. There had been no flying during the day. The observers could not know that recent rain had soaked the airstrips; the soft ground imposing too much drag on the wheels of even the tiny Mentors to permit take-off and too slippery for safe landings of inbound aircraft. By that time the number and type of aircraft on the airfield had been identified, and their positions noted. The number of personnel was more difficult to assess, possibly twenty could have been seen at one time, including men working on trenches and bunkers at the far side of the airfield and at a basic barbed wire fence, hardly an entanglement, along the lower slopes of First Mountain.

The plan of attack was devised by Captain Burls. It would be an old-fashioned, Western Desert-type airfield raid. That meant destroying the aircraft, fuel supplies, ammunition and airfield equipment. Other vehicles or facilities, such as bunkers and trenches, were to be destroyed or rendered useless, the garrison roughed-up and prisoners, especially aircrew, taken for questioning. The reconnaissance and raiding parties, including any wounded (and bodies) were to be evacuated en masse. Anyone separated from the main group or left behind for any reason, such as a lack of space in the helicopters if they were carrying evacuees, or as a rearguard, was to try to reach West Falkland by one of the cached Kleppers. In any case they were to evade capture until recovered by a search and rescue mission, if indeed any men could be spared for what would be an inherently dangerous task and when sorely needed elsewhere for the main landings.

The Islanders could not be evacuated prior to the mission to avoid being punished or used as human shields. Lack of helicopters made that impracticable. Also, being slow-moving civilians, their presence among a withdrawing raiding party, possibly with an aggrieved enemy in hot pursuit, would be an added burden and they might well be injured or killed by crossfire. Protection of the islanders from harm was a major consideration throughout the campaign.

The patrol covering the LUP had also been busy. The map used for planning the mission did not reveal the extent of the pond behind Phillips Cove. It was formed by a stream running downhill from the ridge and dammed by the pebble beach, therefore severely restricting the area on which helicopters could land. During the night two men checked the ground around the pond for firmness and as it was soft then the helicopters would have to hover to let the raiders dismount before returning to *Hermes*. The men also organised themselves as aircraft marshallers. Even in 1982 that meant men wielding torches with red filters; a refinement of the technique evolved by an RAF officer during the Second World War for use by agents in occupied territory. The red lights are almost invisible, even close up, but can be seen for miles through night vision equipment.

When Captain Burls' Warning Order was received at Tactical HQ the flight plans were drawn up. All three remaining Troops would be used, plus a Naval Gunfire Forward Observation (NGFO) team, in reality one officer, Captain Chris Brown RA and a Royal Navy Landing Officer (RNLO), Lieutenant Commander Roger Edwards, to act as guide to the settlement and island terrain. Tasks were then allocated to the Squadron. 18 (Mobility) Troop would deal with the aircraft, vehicles, arms and fuel dumps on the airfield; the men were to prepare improvised demolition charges with wireless-detonated fuses. 16 (Air) Troop, accompanied by the RNLO, would cover the settlement and if possible, seize prisoners. 19 (Mountain) Troop would cover the mortar team and act not only as a quick-reaction force but also as the reserve demolition group, just in case. Major Delves and Captain Brown the NGFO would be between the settlement and eastern end of the airstrip; maintaining contact with all troops and patrols, HMS *Glamorgan*, the helicopters and Tactical HQ (and London) by radio/radio relay. The recce' group from Boat Troop would provide guides for the other parties and, from last light, man an OP overlooking the settlement from Ram's Head.

After dark the patrols on Pebble Island reconnoitred a route between the cove, the mortar position and other sites, the settlement and airfield. Notional ones had already been selected from a large scale map but they had to be thoroughly checked on the ground, with distances paced and compass bearings and back-bearings for each leg double-checked and noted, along with any obstructions such as fences, the wall and any steep-sided gullies.

The settlement and its approaches were also checked. Its layout, or as much as could be discerned at night with low moonlight and scudding clouds, was checked against maps and against the sketches and notes prepared on board. The SAS men also attempted to confirm the presence and nature of any Argentinian defences and alarm-systems. These might be barbed wire entanglements or loose wire strung with empty tins containing pebbles, some possibly set above the height of a browsing sheep, the rest along the ground. The going was checked along each route. It was found to be generally firm apart the most suitable site for the mortar base-plate position which was in a slight hollow with a peaty bottom; a location which was to cause problems during the coming action. The position would also be the post-action rendezvous. It was at GR210105; some 2,000 metres from the airfield, in a re-entrant of the main ridge, just south of Big Pond and about 400 metres below the junction of four fences. The going along the ridge was generally smooth and firm but the side above the ponds was undulating and in the lower reaches boggy. The ponds and marshes were alive with birds, easily disturbed when roosting on the ground or water. The group reassembled at Phillips Cove, conferred, then, apart from sentries, moved into the LUP area to report and lie-up until dark.

Meanwhile, on *Hermes* some intense planning had taken place. The assault phase of the plan was simple. The order of march was to be: Command Group plus Mortar team, followed by Air Troop (settlement) which would peel-off after depositing mortar bombs at the base-plate position, then occupy ground to the right of the Command Group as the Start Line to beat through the settlement. Lieutenant Commander Roger Edwards, the RNLO, would accompany the assault, distinguishing homes from other buildings such as the cow shed or workshop and hopefully calming the islanders and helping them to safety. The Troop would use standard FIBUA (Fighting In Built-Up Areas, now OBUA - Operations in Built Up Areas) techniques to clear the settlement. Air Troop would then form the rearguard to prevent any counter-attacks or follow-up forces during the withdrawal to Phillip's Cove. Mobility Troop would also peel-off from the base-plate position and work through the airfield planting radio-detonated demolition charges on aircraft and dumps.

The raiders would travel in C4 Sea Kings of 846 Squadron, launched as close as possible to Pebble Island from *Hermes*, which would be escorted by HM ships *Glamorgan* and *Broadsword*. C4s could normally carry 27 fully equipped troops for 150 miles and in 1982 were manned by one pilot and a crewman. However, for Special Forces operations they flew with two pilots because of the problems of using

M16 / M203

The American made M16 assault rifle was a favourite with the SAS. It fires the NATO 5.56mm round and is fitted with the M203 40mm grenade launcher.

M16 / 5.56MM RIFLE

Also used was the standard M16 assault rifle which used 5.56mm rounds. Not having the M203 made the weapon was much lighter and easier to handle.

7.62MM GENERAL PURPOSE MACHINE GUN

The 'Gimpy' was a heavy but highly effective weapon with a long range and massive rate of fire. It was carried on the raid without the tripod.

L16 MORTAR 81MM

The L16 was a bulky and heavy weapon to carry but effective as an attack and defence weapon with a maximum range of 5,560 metres.

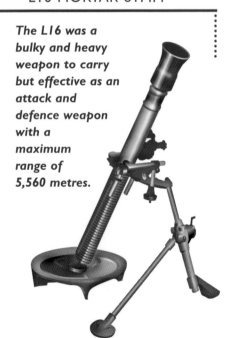

BROWNING FN HIGH POWER PISTOL

The Browning 9mm High Power pistol has had a long standing service in the British Army and is designed to take heavy use.

M72 LAW 66

The LAW 66 was a high explosive anti-tank weapon. It had a prepacked missile, the launch tube was discarded after use.

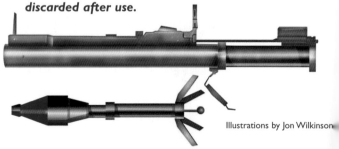

Illustrations by Jon Wilkinson

An SAS soldier armed with the M16 assault rifle fitted with the M203 grenade launcher. Most of the Troopers carried an M16 or a General Purpose Machine Gun and at least one LAW 66. Little webbing was worn so as not inhibit mobility during the raid.

Illustrated by Jon Wilkinson

*The 81mm mortar
being set up for use.*

*Twin carrier tubes for 81mm
mortar bombs.*

night vision low over rough seas, reducing the payload, albeit slightly. Also, strong headwinds and extra low-level flying would further reduce the payload and range, requiring *Hermes* to get closer to Pebble Island than might be considered prudent in view of the air threat. Three Sea Kings were tasked to carry forty-two men; the SAS contingent, Captain Chris Brown and Lieutenant Commander Roger Edwards.

There would also be the mortar weighing 40 kg and more than thirty plastic twin-round bomb carriers at 8 kg each. 'Heavily armed' meant just that. Every SAS man carried an M16 or a GPMG, a Browning 9mm pistol, several magazines or ammunition belts, hand grenades, at least one LAW and many men carried GPMG belts. Little webbing was worn but everyone had their emergency kit. The patrols on Pebble Island were to hide their bergans to improve their mobility on the ground and to reduce weight in the helicopter.[1] While the force was preparing, the patrols on Pebble Island were briefed by radio and made what preparations they could for the raid. This then, would be the largest SAS operation since the Second World War, only exceeding the assault on the Jebel Akhbar in 1956 by a few heads.

On board ship the raiding force prepared their weapons and ammunition. For Captain John Hamilton, officer commanding Mountain Troop, that meant a double load. Mountain Troop had seen action at South Georgia and probably chafed at being in reserve for PRELIM, but in fact had to be ready for several tasks. These included thinking through then planning and preparing to attack the settlement; destroying or damaging aircraft, ground equipment and supplies on the airfield beyond local repair; conducting a counter-attack if the settlement, demolition Troops or HQ were attacked; evacuation of civilians, wounded men and bodies; ambush or anti-ambush attacks of enemy follow-up parties and defence of the landing site to allow evacuation of friendly forces and civilians plus prisoners-of-war. It was a formidable task list and meant carrying a full range of weapons and plenty of ammunition and demolition charges.

The planning session involved many people besides Major Delves. These included Naval staff such as the Staff Navigation Officer (for positioning *Hermes* and her escort group for the helicopter fly-off and recovery), and the Principal Warfare Officer and Navigating Officer of HMS *Glamorgan*, which would provide gunfire support.

NGS - NAVAL GUNFIRE SUPPORT

Naval Gunfire Support is the provision of artillery fire by warships in support of land operations. The main weapon used in the Falklands by the Royal Navy was the 4.5 inch gun, firing illuminating (star-shell), and HE (impact or VT variable-timed fuses) rounds, controlled by observers ashore. On five occasions this was augmented by Sea Slug SAMs! (At one stage it was to be developed to operate surface to surface, albeit with a nuclear warhead.)

A Sea Slug being launched.

The Royal Navy was one of the very few forces anywhere, which practised and had recent experience, of NGS. Within the Task Force it was the responsibility of the Royal Artillery Liaison Officer Naval Gunfire Support (RALONGS), Major Keith Eve, RA. He was one the most experienced NGS officers in the world, with experience gained from the Korean War. That had been followed in 1956 by NGS for Operation MUSKETEER, the assault on Port Said, then the Malayan and Borneo campaigns.

In 1982 NGS was controlled by Naval Gunfire Observation or 'Spotting' Teams, Numbers 1-5, of 148 (Meiktila) Commando Forward Observation Battery, 29 Commando Regiment RA. This was the artillery element of 3 Commando Brigade Royal Marines, in 1982 the major component of the Landing Forces. However, prior to the landing, Major Eve worked in support of precursor operations by Special Forces, so worked with Lieutenant Colonel Rose and Major Thomson. At times he had other masters In a letter to one of the authors he wrote, '*at various times I received orders from C-in-C Fleet* [Northwood], *The Naval task Force Commander* [Admiral Woodward], *Commander 3 Commando Brigade* [Brigadier Julian Thompson], *the Landing Force Commander, and the CRA* [Commander Royal Artillery] *of the Landing Force. However, they were all both sensible and understanding men, and were aware of the difficulties of reconciling often conflicting requirements.*'

RALONGS also worked in close conjunction with the Principal Warfare Officers of ships tasked with providing NGS, co-ordinating fire-plans with NGLOs (one allocated to each designated NGS ship as required) and NGFOs. A Spotting Team, in theory, consisted of an Observation Officer, usually a Captain, RA plus four RA or RN men, all capable of controlling fire if required. 'Fire' included infantry mortars, when the men acted in place of Mortar Fire Controllers, field artillery and ground attack aircraft. Teams could split into two three-man sections or, as happened at Pebble Island, just one observer with a radio.

During the Falklands Campaign, due to shortage of personnel, RALONGS doubled as an NGLO, one of just four available to work with five NGFOs.

NGS requires precise positioning of the ship and then of careful station keeping, all within a few miles of an enemy coast. This requires close co-operation between the NGFOs and the Navigating Officer of the ship providing gunfire support, in this case HMS *Glamorgan*. That meant close scrutiny of naval charts for positioning and maps for plotting the targets. For some campaigns, where time allowed, maps came 'over-printed' with a grid ready for range tables to be added once the NGS Fire Plan had been established. That was not always the case for the Falklands campaign so for Operation PRELIM, *Glamorgan*'s Navigation Officer, Lieutenant Commander Ian Inskip, prepared a superb fire control chart for use by the Principal Weapons Officer, and Captain Christopher Brown RA, the designated Forward Observation Officer for Operation PRELIM and officially known as NGFO5. As the 148 Battery team with the Task Force was under-manned, each Naval Gunfire Observation Officer had one other man in his team, rather than four.

During that day (14 May) Major Eve was on *Glamorgan* planning the Naval Gunfire Support for PRELIM, working with his RN signaller and the ship's weapons officer. He recalled later that at around 1900hrs three war Correspondents; Brian Hanrahan, BBC; Michael Nicholson, ITN, and Martin Cleaver, Press Associates, arrived onboard for a briefing on the operation by the ships' commanding officer, Captain Barrow RN. A naval gunfire support briefing was given by Major Eve, who then snatched some sleep.

He awoke at 0315hrs, and made final checks to maps and the fire-plan for *Glamorgan*'s Operations Room staff.

RAID

HMS *Glamorgan*'s log for 15 May 1982 indicates, '*0400 hrs Arrived on the gun-line...0420hrs Opened fire and 07:45hrs Bombardment complete. Retired at 29 knots! 14 (sic) Aircraft destroyed ashore.*' **Between those times, and beyond the bare bones of these facts, much had happened on Pebble Island.**

Glamorgan left the Task Group at 2000hrs; followed by *Hermes* and *Broadsword* at 2030hrs. As Air Surveillance and Defence ship (albeit with the elderly 35-mile range Sea Slug SAM), *Glamorgan* preceded *Hermes*. *Broadsword* acted as the anti-submarine escort and point anti-aircraft defence ship (with the short -range, vertical launch Sea Wolf system) on the main air threat flank and at some distance away from the other ships' wakes to improve sonar reception. The ships skirted the northern edge of the enemy radar envelope. Fortunately the Argentinians' last Neptune had just been struck off strength, depriving them of long-range radar-surveillance aircraft at just the wrong time.

The wind had increased during the day

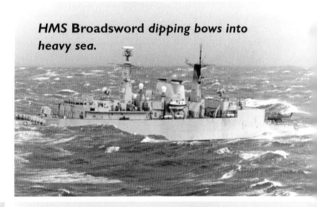

HMS Broadsword *dipping bows into heavy sea.*

HMS Hermes. Taylor Library

HMS Glamorgan *showing 4.5inch gun turret.*

Sea Kings loading the raiding party aboard HMS Hermes.

and by evening was again gusting Force Seven, with accompanying sea states. During the transit to fly-off position the weather created problems for *Hermes'* aircraft-handlers when the Sea Kings were brought up onto the flightdeck from the hangar; problems compounded by a faulty lift mechanism. The weather also forced the Navigating Officer, the Air Planning staff and the helicopter pilots to re-calculate ship and helicopter transit times and fuel consumption. That meant *Hermes* would have to move further west to launch and recover the helicopters twice - a decidedly dangerous situation, given the probable air and submarine threat.

Lieutenant Commander Roger Edwards remarked that,

'[*When we eventually boarded for the mission*] *the aircraft we used had been on deck for a considerable period as we had boarded them once and then had to disembark while* Hermes *steamed flat out to within range of Pebble Island. These aircraft would have remained on deck for the six hours or so until the ship was within range. We went below to the Aircrew Ready Room and spent the time drinking coffee and having a smoke.*'

At that point, *Broadsword*'s Sea Wolf system broke-down. Due to the sea-state the ship had to reduce speed to allow the trainable missile launcher to be locked and disarmed before repairs could take place. That, coupled with strong headwinds, made her fall behind the other ships, causing *Hermes* to slow to ensure she was covered by *Broadsword*'s weapon systems. *Glamorgan* therefore also slowed to keep all three vessels within the Sea Slug engagement zone. Once repairs had been completed the ships headed west at high speed.

Despite careful route-planning, the ships were plotted by the Argentinians in

Trainable Sea Wolf SAM launcher. MD Thomas

Stanley and were reported as moving from *en posicion general 49°30' Sur* [South] */50°30' Oeste* [West] ... *se aproximaron en la noche a la boca del estracho de San Carlos* (within the radar shadow). Stanley alerted Lieutenant Marega to the reappearance of three ships heading west past the northern coast of Pebble Island. (The Argentinian GHQ may have assessed these movements over the previous two nights to be associated with the radar picket north of the island.)

At 0200hrs *Hermes* reduced speed and launched the Sea Kings twenty-five minutes later and by a variety of signal routes, that information was passed to Boat Troop on Pebble Island. The carrier and *Broadsword* retired to loiter outside the radar envelope, ready to return to recover the helicopters for refuelling for the recovery sortie.

On *Glamorgan* Major Eve made final adjustments to maps and the Fireplan prepared for the ship's Operations Centre staff. He also had a final word with Lieutenant Commander Inskip. During one of the planning sessions Eve found a discrepancy of 400 yards between naval charts and land maps due to changes of grid origin; once that had been detected and allowed for, the first naval gunfire support salvo onto *Borbon* was to prove remarkable. *Glamorgan* closed to her designated Fire Support Area, slightly north-west of, and some six miles from, *Borbon* to allow for the strong westerly wind and provide maximum burn-time for

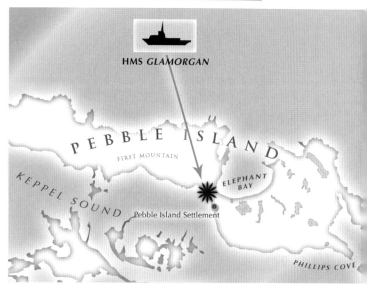

HMS *GLAMORGAN*'S DESIGNATED FIRE SUPPORT AREA

Star Shell flares which are ignited and ejected at the top of the shell's trajectory.

After the Sea Kings left the immediate area of *Hermes* they descended to low level and headed for the east end of Pebble Island. Roger Edwards again:

> 'The weather generally was very cold and foggy for that time of year and did cause some problems landing folks ashore. On the night of the raid it was generally good visibility but with a gale from the WNW. I can remember quite a large sea running as every now and again a breaking crest could be seen level with the door of the Sea King - we were quite low!'

Meanwhile, on Pebble Island, Boat Troop, less a two-man observation post watching the approaches from the airfield and settlement, had re-assembled at Phillips Cove. While his men enjoyed a quick brew, made for them by the landing site guards, Captain Burls briefed those not keeping watch on what had been seen of *Borbon* and on the routes and obstacles. He then allocated tasks. First was nomination, or rather confirmation, of the helicopter marshalling team. He confirmed that the evacuation landing zone would be close to the mortar base plate position. The Sea Kings would fly to the Cove and then hug the ridge-crests looking for the marshal's torches.

Secondly, guides were appointed for the various assault groups and the position of the mortar base-plate position briefed and located on maps. Reinforcements were sent to the OP by the settlement, carrying as much ammunition as could be spared for GPMGs, to disrupt any attempt at interference if the helicopters were detected on their way in to the cove.

Captain Burls prepared to brief the incoming Squadron but they were later than expected. The helicopters arrived at 0350hrs, homing in on the marshal's torches in turn and hovering, wheels barely touching the ground, to unload the heavily laden raiding party. '*We landed facing North,*' recalled Roger Edwards, '*on the left of the valley so that on exit we went downhill away from the rotors.*' A brief message announcing safe arrival was passed up the chain of command. The helicopters returned to *Hermes* to refuel and, as time was so short, to start the evacuation. There was never any question of waiting on the carrier for a recovery call.

On *Glamorgan* Major Eve and his navy signaller, Leading Radio Operator Wilcox, had everything ready. The naval gunfire support part of the Fire Plan, code-named Antarctic Fox, could be initiated whenever it was needed; the guns were ready to be loaded with the first

	(a) TARGET No.	(b) DESCRIPTION	(c) LOCATION	(d) ALT?	(e) REMARKS
	ZJ5004	FIRST MT	UD 149 148	900	ON CALL PREDICT
	ZJ5005		UD 165 145	450	PREDICT
	ZJ5006		UD 178 141	100	ON CALL PREDICT
	ZJ5007		UD 184 126	75	" " "
	ZJ5008	FIRE SP BASE	UD 200 110	50	" " "
	ZJ5009	BASE PLATE LS	UD 210 105	25	" " "

The fire plan.

rounds (Star-shell), and all targets were plotted, and checked. After sorting out a slight confusion over radio frequencies and learning of the successful insertion of the raiding party, Major Eve opened up on the naval gunfire officer's radio net at 0400hrs, informing Captain Brown that *Glamorgan* was on the Gun-line.

In reply Captain Brown-NGFO5- advised him that naval gunfire would not be required until 0630hrs due to the delay in landing. However, as there were now friendly forces ashore who might require it at any time, and as the ship was in hostile waters, *Glamorgan* stood to Action Stations. Major Eve stood ready to receive situation reports or calls for illumination or fire support. Around that time (0410hrs) *Glamorgan*'s Principal Weapons Officer advised RALONGS that, as the visibility was good, the ship would have to come off the Gun Line at 0730hrs, (shortly after sunrise at 0728hrs) and depart the Fire Support Area to gain the safety of the British air patrol umbrella, some thirty miles away, by daylight. Captain Brown requested the ship be ready to fire the first rounds at 0700hrs. RALONGS acknowledged, indicating that *Glamorgan* was ready to execute Fireplan Antarctic Fox.

It was now 0415hrs, just over three

TARGETS FOR FIRE PLAN - ANTARCTIC FOX

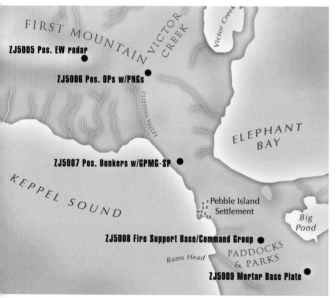

hours before sunrise. H-Hour, the time the assault force would cross the start-line, had been set for 0630hrs, so the raiders had to reach their targets, mount the attack and return very quickly indeed. It should be remembered that many men of D Squadron had been in action under severe weather conditions on South Georgia, and had then lived in some discomfort on board ship. It is also worth bearing in mind that such a large raid, even on exercise, was a very unusual, if not unique event, for an entire modern-day SAS Squadron to undertake.

At Phillips Cove the incoming troops rapidly cleared the immediate area of the LZ and clustered at the top of the valley above the Cove, covered by Boat Troop's sentries. Captain Burls quickly updated Major Delves, WOII Gallagher and the troop leaders. He, in turn, was briefed by his commanding officer. The plan of attack was rapidly reviewed so that everyone was up to speed with information gathered by Boat Troop.

The plan, essentially, followed the outline set on *Hermes*, with one change. Boat Troop, whose task was to act as guides and provide the covering party for the settlement, would also be the rearguard during the withdrawal. Mountain Troop was to cover the mortar position and evacuation landing zone, while Mobility Troop was to be the airfield assault force. The change was that Air Troop, plus RNLO, would not now assault the settlement but provide a barrier between it and the airfield. HQ and Captain Brown would be in what had been designated as the Fire Support Base, forward of the mortar position, close to the barrier and able to observe the airfield area. The Start Line for the airfield assault would be a fence running between the pond near Elephant Beach to the settlement. The withdrawal rendezvous would be at the mortar base plate position.

THE REVISED PLAN AND ROUTES

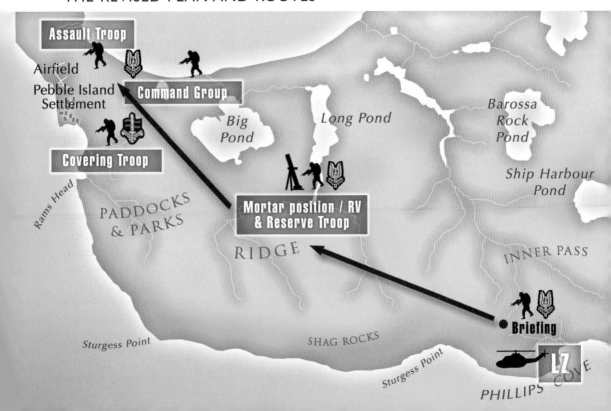

There was a change to the original approach march. During the flight Major Delves had revised the timetable to allow for the various delays. Here he threw caution to the wind but it was a calculated risk. Instead of the Troops and HQ group taking separate routes, everyone would head for the settlement at high speed and in single file, himself in front with Captain Burls as guide. The order of march would be; HQ group; mortar team; Air Troop; remainder of Boat Troop; Mountain Troop; Mobility Troop.

The Squadron took off, led by Captain Burls, compass in hand and counting paces, moving quickly despite their heavy loads. A rising westerly wind scattered the light cloud cover, providing intermittent light from the moon, in its last quarter. *'There was good visibility'*, according to Roger Edwards, *'First Mountain could be seen as a big black shape ahead of us.'*

At 0610hrs the mortar base plate position was reached. The mortar team peeled-off and started to set-up the weapon. As the other raiders passed, each dropped their bomb-carriers in a pile. The base-plate was dropped, the barrel fitted, the bipod erected, sights clipped in place and the sighting-post set-up; the mortar was ready to fire by 0615hrs. While the mortarman checked the sights his colleagues stacked the bomb-carriers in two piles, parachute illumination and HE, unscrewing the caps of each tube to expose the rounds, ready for quick withdrawal.

The HQ Group and Air Troop reached their position by the slope leading down to the settlement, where Air Troop sited GPMGs to cover the settlement and the surrounding slopes. They were in luck. The wind was in their faces so their scent, probably fairly rich after some weeks with limited access to showers, did not reach the sheepdog kennels. Also, just below them (or so it seemed) they could hear a generator running, masking all other sounds. Only the day before Second Lieutenant Castro had asked the settlement's mechanic, Norman Morrison, to do a small welding job. It may seem strange that he agreed to help them, but as he said later, it was, *'better than them having a go and ruining the gear.'* Norman had the workshop generator running all day while he was doing the task and in the evening he forgot to switch it from 'RUN' to 'TIMER', so it kept running through the night instead of switching itself off automatically. None of the Argentinians seemed to notice!

At the final rendezvous near the OP, Sergeant Major Gallagher, who was checking-in each Troop as it passed, realised that Mobility Troop had not arrived and immediately advised Major Delves. A quick wireless check revealed that at some point the Troop Commander had lost sight of the man in front. His Troop was somewhere down near the ponds, lost. Major Delves called Captain Hamilton, OC Mountain Troop, who, apart from listening into the Squadron net, had just been told by his 'tail-end Charlie' that he was not being followed,

First Mountain looming over the airfield. R Evans

although he could not recall exactly when or where the missing men had last been noticed.

There was no time to lose. As the designated reserve for the attack on the airfield, Mountain Troop had not only been as fully briefed as Mobility Troop but had already discussed how they would handle the task. They had, obviously, been issued with plastic explosive, wireless detonators, and wrapping materials. The main reason why the troop had been designated as the reserve assault force was due to the fact that one of their number, Corporal Raymond Armstrong, a former member of the Royal Green Jackets, was a demolitions expert. He and other members of the troop had made up a number of demolition charges to deal with aircraft and other possible airfield targets.

Led by a delighted Captain Hamilton the Troop took-off for the airfield and were in their forming up position behind the Start Line just before 0700hrs.

Mobility Troop was the last to leave Phillips Cove and being at the end of the column and due to shortage of guides were not allocated one. (There were only four Boat Troop men, one two-man patrol which had been near the airfield and only two who had been all the way to the far side of the airfield. Five groups/Troops required guides). The other Troops had raced off, crossing the various fences and the wall almost without pause to avoid losing sight of the men in front. There was no tactical crossing of obstacles; if the 'Boss' and Ted Burls hadn't been whacked getting over them then there had obviously been no-one lurking nearby with malice aforethought.

Mobility Troop's OC, however, operated by the book. As the leading man reached an obstacle everyone adopted all-round defence. The fence - they never reached the wall - was crossed in accordance with British Army fieldcraft training; weapon made safe, magazine off, on the ground pointing away from the soldier, cross the obstacle, retrieve the weapon, fit the magazine, cock the piece and apply the safety catch, take up a defensive position. As a result, while traversing the undulating terrain of the plateau, the Mobility Troop first fell behind then veered off route, went too far down hill and became lost among the broken ground near the wetlands. Worse, someone dropped a weapon near a fence in the bogs by Big Pond. Despite an urgent search it was not found. During that process Major Delves contacted the commanding officer and was told of the situation. As time was running out Mobility were allocated the reserve task and told to follow the fence uphill to the crest of the ridge, turn right, and find the mortar site. (Quite unmistakable from the flash every time a bomb was fired, despite the weapon being in a dip.)

The bog area near Big Pond. Allan White

77

*A Shorts
Skyvan which
was destroyed
with small
arms fire.*

PREFECTURA NAVAL ARGENTINA

PA-54

Illustrated by Jon Wilkinson

While heading for the airfield Captain Hamilton and Corporal Armstrong had decided to use their limited supply of charges on the Pucaras and any arms and fuel dumps, while their colleagues tackled the Mentors and the Skyvan with small arms, 40mm grenades, and Light Anti-armour Weapons (LAWs). The LAW is a High Explosive Anti-Tank (HEAT) rocket fitted with a shaped-charge warhead. When the rocket strikes the target an instantaneous fuse ignites the charge, turning it into a narrow jet of molten copper alloy. This will penetrate tank armour up to 305mm (12 inches) thick, incinerating the crew, devastating radios and instruments, and detonating unprotected ammunition. LAWs are less effective against aircraft unless fired at fuel tanks, an engine block, or the junction of the main wing spar and the fuselage. Against a twin-engined aircraft such as a Pucara the best effect is likely to be obtained by firing at the nose from dead ahead. That would destroy the instrument panel, and probably detonate the explosive charges in the ejection seats.

*A LAW 66 in the
process of being fired
from a crouched
position.*

*The LAW flip up
rear site which
had to be used in
darkness.*

50
100
150
200
250
300
350

For single-engined aircraft such as Mentors the jet will destroy the propeller hub, the engine and possibly the control panel. For a Skyvan it can also be used from dead ahead to destroy the control panel or, better still, aimed from the flank at the junction of the shoulder-mounted wing and fuselage to damage or destroy the main spar, rupture and ignite the fuel tanks. Due to the weapon's delayed-arming mechanism it cannot be used less than 10 yards from a target. Even at that range a night head-on shot against a small target such as the nose of a small aircraft, seen in the wavering light of parachute flares, would be tricky. There is also the problem of back-blast: highly dangerous for 15 yards behind the firer. The flash will also degrade night-vision for some minutes for anyone within the immediate area unless a warning is yelled by the firer, as is taught in some forces.

At 0700hrs RALONGS reminded Captain Brown, and through him Major Delves, that *Glamorgan* had to cease fire at 0730. The reply was that that was noted and the airfield assault Troop were only now in their forming up positions. The first salvoes were to be Star Shells over target ZJ5007, the approximate area of the Marines' bunkers by the Marble Shanty Track, not high explosive onto target ZJ5004 (the summit of First Mountain, as a diversionary target) as planned. That required *Glamorgan*'s gun crew to change the ammunition loaded into the automatic feed mechanism, which was carried out quickly. The scene was now set for the raid.

Captain Brown called for Star Shell at 0719hrs. It was delivered at 0722hrs and continued with rounds fired at 15 second intervals until high explosive was called for. The first flares immediately revealed the number of aircraft to be attacked (eleven) and their disposition around the airfield, requiring some hasty re-thinking on the part of Captain Hamilton and his men.

THE PROGRESSION OF THE ATTACK

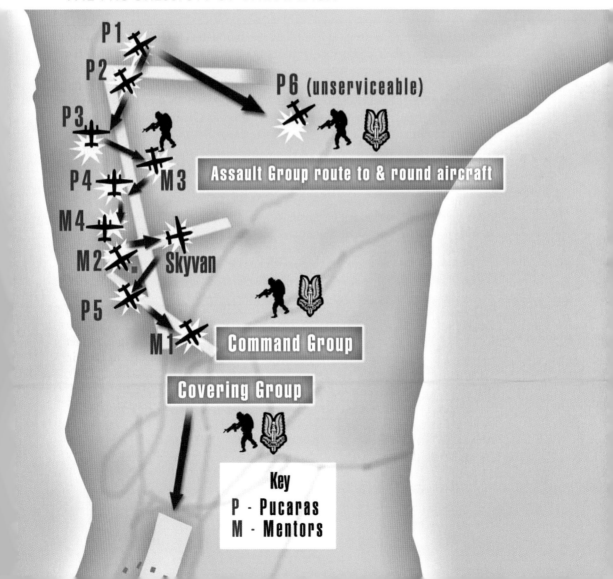

P1

P2

P6 (unserviceable)

P3

Assault Group route to & round aircraft

P4 M3

M4

M2 Skyvan

P5

M1 Command Group

Covering Group

Key
P - Pucaras
M - Mentors

It also produced what Captain Brown later described as, '*an immediate response from the enemy, who were obviously forewarned, and were in the hills above Pebble Island Settlement*'. (There is no note of any such response in the Argentinian Separata No 20; but it is reasonable to assume that a spooked sentry may have fired in reaction to the flare.)

In reply to the enemy intervention Major Delves, through Captain Brown, called for high explosive and via the SAS net, for Para-Illumination rounds from the mortar. The high explosive was delivered onto target ZJ5007, with, as has been noted above, commendable accuracy, given that there had been no ranging shots. Target ZJ50007 was the col on the eastern flank of First Mountain, which dominated the airfield area and was the obvious place for defences such as GPMG - operating in the sustained fire role - mortar and recoilless rifle pits. According to Captain Brown, the whole of the ridge was neutralised by spreading fire, with the rounds being 'walked' downhill towards the settlement. It was checked just as Mountain Troop reached the edge of the airfield without having come under enemy fire-effective or otherwise; the few Marines on the airfield having been effectively suppressed.

Whilst Corporal Armstrong and Captain Hamilton tackled the Pucaras, their colleagues raced to their designated targets and set about them with M16/M203s, GPMGs and LAWs. Everyone realised they were perpetuating the work of such SAS legends as Bob Bennett, Johnny Cooper, Dave Kershaw and above all, Paddy Main; destroyers of aircraft par excellence, despite having different weapons.

DISABLING AIRCRAFT

In 1941, at RAF Heliopolis, L Detachment SAS Brigade learned how to sabotage aircraft and airfield equipment to maximum effect. Jock Lewes, David Stirling, Bill Cumper and other 'Originals' were taught by a Scottish RAFVR engineering officer, father of one of this book's authors, and his long-serving (and long suffering) Flight Sergeant.

Between 1945 and the Pebble Island Raid in 1982, British SAS troops, as far as can be discerned from open sources, did not attack aircraft or airfields but the basic techniques did not change over the years. If aircraft cannot be destroyed outright a number of the same type can be immobilised by demolishing a common item on each, making cannibalisation difficult or impossible, depending on the spares situation on the airfield. (Hence the need for observers and CTR teams to locate the engineering workshop and stores on a target airfield.) Nose-wheel tyres or instrument panels can be shattered by small arms fire. Landing-gear leg hinges can be destroyed with small demolition charges or damaged by grenades thus collapsing the aircraft and probably causing structural damage. Improvised airfields such as Pebble Island are rarely supplied with a mobile crane, making recovery and repair of 'dropped' aircraft almost impossible.

Corporal Armstrong worked his way round the aircraft, distributing his charges with care. The Pucaras, including the ditched A-523, had charges placed inside the undercarriage wells of the engine nacelles, or were strapped to undercarriage leg-joints with adhesive tape.

HMS Glamorgan *providing Naval* **Gun Support.**

The four Mentors, A-401, A-408, A-411 and A-412 each received two charges, one under the port tail-plane, the other under the engine, inside the nose-wheel bay. Aviation fuel and ammunition 'dumps' could not be located.[1] Several drums of JP-1 were found, some by accident, when they were hit by small-arms fire. That included those in the small *depositivo combustivo* by the Fire Tender Hut.

Lieutenant Marega had placed a small night guard of six Marines on the airfield, two in the fire tender hut and four in a roamer patrol. When the first flares ignited, the guards in the hut telephoned Lieutenant Marega, who had heard *Glamorgan's* gunfire, he had already realised the expected attack had started. The other officers in the School/Mess were also awake and Lieutenant Castro telephoned a contact report to the CCM in Stanley.

Argentinian accounts differ from the time the British high explosive shells started to thump First Mountain but it appears as though Lieutenant Marega, a Marine NCO and an engineer Corporal headed first for the DFCC to test the firing circuit and then attach the detonating wires and cord to the detonator and igniter. The Corporal remained in the centre while the two Marines, weapons in hand, crept up the slope leading to the airfield and peered over the edge. Due to the terrain they had to stand to see anything and witnessed a number of shadowy figures running towards and around the parked aircraft, pausing only to fire weapons or throw hand grenades.

The two Marines made their way towards the fire tender hut. They were spotted and challenged by the two guards, and went inside. Everyone crouched on the floor as there were small arms rounds cracking past the hut at odd intervals. The guards reported that they were huddled in the hut, more or less out of the wind, when they were galvanised by the distant blast of *Glamorgan*'s first rounds. Each shot briefly lit up the night sky to the northeast. Those first rounds were followed by a barrage of star-shell and then mortar, flares and HE shells bursting apparently above the guards on First Mountain. These explosions were succeeded by streams of GPMG tracer rounds going into and through aircraft, small arms fire, grenade and LAW blasts. The SAS mortar flare illumination was intermittent. Every two or three rounds the mortar base-plate sank into the soft soil of the dell and had to be hauled out, re-positioned and the barrel re-aligned.

One of the 40mm grenades caused an own goal; Corporal Davey, Mountain Troop, was hit in the leg by a splinter. He was immediately attended to by his patrol commander, Staff Sergeant Philip Currass, D Squadron's Royal Army Medical Corps specialist. (Currass was also a fully-trained SAS operator, boat-handler, troop 2i/c and patrol leader). Corporal Davey was more annoyed than hurt and after treatment was able to hobble back to the rendezvous, where he was again examined, given further attention to his leg and sent back to the mortar pit with an escort-cum-guide; both men disappointed at missing the action.

A further spectacular effect occurred when something, a 7.62mm GPMG, 5.56mm M16 rounds or grenade splinter, breached the fuel tank of Lieutenant Pereya's Mentor A-401, aircraft, releasing fuel onto the grass. Another something, perhaps a tracer round, parachute flare, LAW rocket or 40mm grenade fragment, ignited the petrol soaking into the grass strip. The fuel around the aircraft erupted in flames. The Argentinian roamer patrol was spotted near the Guard Hut, where Lieutenant Marega was trying to figure out what was happening. He ordered the patrol to take some chemical fire extinguishers, standard equipment for a light aircraft base, and tackle the blaze. When some of the raiders saw the figures emerge from the hut carrying the bulky objects they opened fire on them. The marines dropped their loads, took cover as best they could by the hut and returned fire at shadowy, half glimpsed figures racing around the airfield. The SAS raiders returned fire but for only a brief period, as the Marines' shooting was not effective.[2] The defensive fire seems to have continued for some time, possibly until the Marines ran out of ammunition or their ardour was suppressed by accurate return fire. Several accounts state that as the raiders withdrew, two Argentinians, presumably Lieutenant Marega, and an NCO, attempted to intervene. They reportedly yelled at their men to rally and open fire and opened fire themselves in the general direction of the vague shapes seen amongst the smoke from the explosions, fires, flares and by the light of the intermittent moonlight. Their efforts were silenced by a blizzard of small-arms fire and M-203 grenades. Roger Edwards recalled that, *'there was a very short firefight on the strip and a couple of Argentinians were slightly wounded, I do not remember anyone being killed.'*

The SAS barrier group did not open fire although they were ready to do so if any Argentinians attempted to advance up the slope in front of them leading to the airstrips. None did. Discretion was the better part of valour that night and in any case the only 'tooth-arm' officer, Lieutenant Marega, was on the airfield.

The last shot, so to speak, fired by defenders caused the worst injury suffered by the SAS. Just as Corporal Armstrong was trying to attach a charge to the sixth Pucara, A–523, down by the eastern end of the northerly airstrip, Lieutenant Marega ordered the detonation of the airfield demolition charges. Corporal Armstrong was blown off his feet, severely shaken, and was deafened for some days afterwards but was otherwise unhurt.

Lieutenant Marega had assessed that the British might be about to land Hercules transports carrying a follow-up force onto the airfield and intended to deny them use of the main airstrip. The result was a considerable tribute to the skill of the combat engineers. All of the charges went off, blowing neat, deep craters. Unfortunately the Skyvan aircraft was parked over the middle of a line of charges and destroyed.

One Argentinian account is more flamboyant;

'repentinamente se produjo una gran explosion, pues en medio de la

operación, el canonazo de un buque britanico dio en una de las camaras de voladura que los Infantrie de Marina Argentinos habian instalado para destruir la pista en caso de ocupacon de la base por fuerzas enemigas.'

The demolition charges also caused further minor casualties. According to Roger Edwards,

> *'when the demolition team were withdrawing from the strip a command-detonated mine was set off slightly injuring two of the boys (ears rang for a week I was told).'*

Corporal Bunker, Mountain Troop, was blown over and concussed by the blast; he had already been injured in the Wessex crashes on Fortuna Glacier. He, too, was helped back to the mortar pit, where the reserve troop had helped extricate the weapon and collect any unopened carriers. Uncased rounds were then fired-off and the empty cases left behind, trophies for the garrison, later to be requisitioned by security personnel.

Time was getting was short; sunrise would be at 0728hrs but there would be light before that to assist a determined attack by Pucaras from Stanley by an Exocet-armed aircraft from the Argentinian mainland. Therefore the pick-up, return flight and departure of the Carrier Group had to be completed as soon as possible. On Captain Hamilton's signal the demolition charges were blown and more small arms, GPMG and LAW fire opened on aircraft lacking demolition charges. The results, coupled with the wavering light from the star shells and mortar bombs, were spectacular. A signal was sent to *Hermes* stating the attack had been successful and requesting evacuation. The carrier and *Broadsword* were moving towards the helicopter recovery position. That decision had been taken some time before, following urgent discussions between various naval command and staff officers, Tactical HQ and Major Delves, since the delays, coupled with distance, the weather and the approach of sunrise indicated an early departure.

THE ROUTE OF WITHDRAWAL AND LIFT-OFF

Airfield

ebble Island
Settlement

Rams Head

PADDOCKS & PARKS

Big Pond

Long Pond

Barossa Rock Pond

Ship Harbour Pond

Raiders withdrawal route

Emergency RV & Sea King Landing Zone

LZ RIDGE

INNER PASS

Sea Kings route inbound

Sturgess Point

SHAG ROCKS

rgess Point

COVE

AIRCRAFT DESTROYED - TEN OR ELEVEN?

Most English language accounts of the raid state that eleven aircraft were destroyed. However, all Argentinian sources, including the official FAA website and those of other Argentinian armed forces and the PNA, admit to only ten; five Pucaras, four Mentors and a Skyvan. To quote, *'en seta operation, la FAA perdió los IA-58 Pucará matrículas A-502, A-520, A-526, A-529, A-552.*

The discrepancy is to due to Pucara A-523 having been struck-off the strength following its hard landing. The SAS attacked it, however, unaware of its state, and it was seriously damaged.

Lit by the glare of flares and a burning aircraft the raiders withdrew. The garrison did not appear to have any plan for dealing with a raid, although someone managed to transmit a message which eventually found its way to the command centre in Stanley. There was not much that could be done to help due to the lack of night-flying equipment at the air bases and in the helicopters, Pucaras and Mentors and even less experience of night anti-helicopter operations by any of the aircrew. The clumsy chain of command at *Borbon*, naval aviation, marines, air force and coastguard, hardly helped matters. There was no lack of courage, but also no experience of being under fire and no tradition of airfield defence as taught by the RAF Regiment and practised by all ranks on British military airfields during Tactical Evaluation exercises.

When the entire raiding party had been checked through the rendezvous and assembled close to the mortar pit, they took off eastwards; exhaustion overcome by the adrenalin 'high' of a close quarters contact. The raiders travelled in a fast moving column of Troops, with an advance guard to deal with an ambush and a rear guard trotting behind in case of pursuit. Under Captain Brown's control, *Glamorgan* laid down a curtain of fire onto First Mountain which was gradually 'walked' westwards along the north flank as if covering a withdrawal towards the area around Marble Shanty.

The Sea Kings were on their way, flying in from the Ship Harbour area to meet the withdrawing troops. This was a considerable risk. No-one could be sure the garrison did not have 81 or 120mm mortars, an ideal method of illuminating, then harassing withdrawing troops and deadly against a helicopter landing zone, especially one being used for a 'hot extraction'.

The Sea Kings spotted and headed towards the marshaller's torches. A rolling rendezvous was achieved about two miles from the airfield; a last-minute barrage from *Glamorgan* was laid down between the SAS party and the settlement. It ceased at 0745hrs, once the helicopters signalled that the raiding party had embarked. *Glamorgan* then departed with all speed.

The raiding force boarded the helicopters and returned to *Hermes*, which was loitering, bows down wind, ready to turn about and depart at high speed once the Sea Kings were secured on deck.

A relieved Roger Edwards later recalled that, *'we got back to* Hermes *in time for breakfast and she was soon speeding east just as fast as she could go.'*

AFTERMATH

The raiders had departed Pebble Island, leaving behind a bewildered Borbon garrison and a petrified population. The CANA officers radioed a situation report to the command centre at Stanley and to *BAM Condor*, alerting them to the attack and the fact that 'many aircraft' had been damaged or destroyed. They were told to sit tight and await help.

After the gunfire ceased the garrison slowly sorted themselves out and again the complicated chain of command did not help. Eventually a patrol of marines, including combat engineers to search for delayed action-bombs or booby-traps, moved gingerly out of the settlement and onto the airfield. They were followed at a discrete distance by the air and groundcrew. All were appalled at the damage.

Every aircraft had been damaged beyond local repair. The Skyvan was little more than two wings and stub of fuselage complete with a tail; the rest was simply a blob of melted alloy on scorched grass. One Mentor was burned out, while others and the Pucaras were lying at drunken angles due to collapsed undercarriages. Many aircraft were

The broken remains of the Skyvan.

Pucara A-502. Note the triple ejection racks under outer wings. Ian Howat

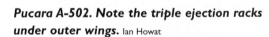

A closer view of another Pucara showing the damage done by small arms fire. On the far left, the wreckage of a Mentor lays in the grass.

riddled by small arms, shrapnel from 40mm grenades or LAW rockets. At the intersection of airstrips the demolition charges had performed faithfully, a tribute, if not a welcome one, to the marine engineers who laid them. They had created massive craters, closing the airstrips to any type of aircraft then on the islands.

The air threat to the landings at San Carlos, and to the radar picket off Pebble Island, had been eliminated.

The raid demonstrated the ability of British Special Forces to strike more or less at will. The officers manning the Argentinian CCM command post in Stanley were far from stupid and despite the lack any significant Special Forces capability

An aerial photograph showing craters in the airstrip blown by the Argentine Marine Engineers during the attack.

Fleet Air Arm Museum

Pucara A-529. Ian Howat

Mentor 408. Ian Howat

Mentor 412. Ian Howat

An aerial photograph showing the extent of the damage the morning after the raid. Fleet Air Arm Museum

A reconnaissance photograph taken by a Sea Harrier the morning after the attack. Fleet Air Arm Museum

(*Buzos* excepted) understood the principles of their use.[1] The helicopter flights plotted by the Argentinians had made the command staff realise that British 'commandos' might be anywhere. For all they knew there might still be some on Pebble Island, ready to act as pathfinders for a parachute or helicopter assault to establish a forward operating base. They might yet set up amphibious landing markers on Elephant Beach for a follow-up force to the raid or on any other beach around the coast. There could be a raid on any outpost or OP, or even on the command and supply centre in Stanley; echoes of such SAS and SBS exploits in North Africa and around the Mediterranean during the Second World War.[2] The CCM was determined to interfere with this issue and to scour the area of probable British landing sites. That meant deploying troops experienced in patrolling and counter-insurgency or similar operations.

The *Gendarmería Nacional* (GN) had the personnel. There was already a GN presence on the islands and that was augmented and then divided to form an anti-SAS/SBS unit. This was *Escuadron Alacran de la Compania de Tropas Especiales 601 de Gendarmería Nacional* (Scorpion Squadron, 601 Special Forces Company).[3] It consisted of a small HQ team (*Comando del Escuadron*), a vague-titled *Seccion de Empleos Especiales* (SEE), possibly for counter-intelligence (interrogation) purposes, and the *Seccion de Tiradores Especiales*; Special Riflemen Section. The unit assembled at Rio Gallegos on 27 May and moved the following day. Unfortunately, that same day seven key personnel were killed in a helicopter crash on Mount Kent. The unit had little chance to operate in its intended role. Later, however it saw action when elements were deployed forward of the Argentinian front line, patrolling against 3 Commando Brigade's recce' patrols, including those mounted by D (Patrols) Company of 3 Battalion, The Parachute Regiment, in the Murrell Bridge area.

The effects of D Squadron's raid went beyond just physical damage; few Argentinians on the Malvinas slept soundly from that day on until after the

Pucara A527 after further demolition due to safety reasons. Ian Howat

surrender. Argentinian morale had been severely dented but strangely the raid also served to stiffen resolve in some quarters. As it was they left a small garrison on Pebble Island, including naval aircrew. This was to have tragic consequences for the Task Force.

The Argentinian Marines checked the area for stay-behind parties, checked the airfield for unexploded ordnance and collected the empty LAW launch-tubes, numerous small-arms cartridge cases and live rounds in addition to what appeared to be discarded wrappers from demolition charges.[4]

While the damage was being assessed another patrol of marines and combat engineers carefully searched the area around the settlement, alert for ambushes. They could not be sure that a force of 'commandos' was not lurking in the gorse, ready to mount an attack or open fire with machine guns. There was also the spine-chilling realisation for the young marines that they might walk into a Claymore mine ambush; a horrifying thought which made them walk very carefully indeed, particularly in and around gorse. They were well-trained; moving slowly, weapon slung, eyes down, right hand at arm's length with a length of fence-wire held lightly between two fingers as primitive but effective trip-wire detectors. That slowed the search considerably but eventually it was realised that the raiders had withdrawn, at least from the immediate area.

The marines and engineers had a scratch meal and a mug of comforting if weak *maté* tea, and started work on strengthening the primitive defences just in case another attack materialised. It is worth recalling that this was a very small force, around seventy men. They were mainly young marine *colimbi*, conscripts, with some older NCOs and officers. The *Infanteria de Marina* had not seen action, ashore or afloat, since the early 1800s. None of the marines therefore had been in action or under fire, few had ever lived in the field for more than a few days, and even fewer had experienced such inhospitable terrain and a truly foreign country.

Shortly after first light two Pucaras flew over the settlement, carrying what appeared to be bombs or napalm tanks.[5] They circled the area and surveyed possible landing sites on beaches before returning to Goose Green. There the crews confirmed that the remains of eleven aircraft could be seen, also some burnt-out fuel drums, and large craters.

Later, at 1030hrs, more engine noise heralded the arrival of help - of sorts. It was a Chinook, serial H-39, from Stanley bringing FAA officers to inspect the damage. It also carried fifty men from 601 Commando Company. Their task was to conduct a sweep of the area and to search the rest of the island. The Chinook had barely touched down, and the FAA and Commando men dismounted, when a mob of air and ground crew took it by storm. The fact that none of the garrison had been killed was irrelevant; the Argentinians recognised that the presence of the families in their midst had prevented the British from shooting-up every building with machine-guns, mortars and LAWs, or from aerial or artillery bombardment. The Chinook needed two sorties to evacuate the FAA and PNA aircrew, and all of the groundcrew, and to collect the, *material inglés abandonado*.[6]

The commandos searched the same areas as the marines and made a helicopter-mounted survey of the rest of the island. They paid particular attention to Marble Shanty and Pebble Cove, and even contemplated crossing to Keppel Island, but in the end found nothing of interest.

The raid had been a resounding success. For the loss of only one man slightly wounded and another temporarily deafened, the SAS had disabled or destroyed six Pucaras, four Mentors and a Skyvan. The SAS had not only wiped out a vital Argentinian reconnaissance and attack force, it had also destroyed the remaining transport aircraft capable of landing on Pebble Island. This effectively denied the Argentinian CCM the use of Pebble Island as a forward operating base as the garrison could not be reinforced or supplied.

The raid reduced the Pucara force on the Islands to eleven. The Argentinians immediately reinforced the detachment at Goose Green which confirms the importance they attached to the Pucaras for countering an amphibious landing. At 10:25 hrs on 15 May the FAA ordered BAM Rio Gallegos the despatch of four Pucaras to Goose Green as soon as possible. At 14:43hrs the mission, call-sign 'Pocker', departed. It was escorted by a FAA Mitsubishi MU-2B acting as navigation leader and radio-relay ship.

An uncomfortable consequence of the raid for the islanders was their confinement to the Big House. The remaining officers on the island, possibly prodded by the remote but ever-vigilant Major Dowling, suspected that someone in the settlement had been in contact with British Special Forces before or during the raid. According to Ken Bernsten, interviewed by Allan White in February 2006, the garrison's suspicions were due to Norman Morrison's generator having been running when the SAS raid took place. Ken recalled;

> '...the next morning the Argies rounded all the locals up and accused them of knowing that the raid was going to take place and that Norman had deliberately left the generator running so the noise would mask any noise made by the approaching raiders.'

For this reason they decided to incarcerate the civilians in the Big House, and place them under armed guard. The islanders and evacuees, including the very pregnant Fiona Clarke and seven children, moved out of their homes and the Argentinian garrison moved in. At last they had boiling water for their *maté*, once the mysteries of peat-burning Rayburn stoves had been tackled, if not altogether solved effectively; hence the subsequent fire which burned down a house leaving nothing standing but the foundations, a water pipe and tap.

The civilians were initially held in close confinement. However, due to their complaints, the agonised bellowing of un-milked cows and Argentinian common sense, their situation improved. Everyone was allowed to gather food, to tend chickens, refuel the generators, check the sheep and cows, but always with an 'escort'.

When not outside the islanders were guarded day and night by marines. One guard, a conscript named Jorge, lived in the Big House all the time as he spoke fluent English and could understand all that was said. According to Raymond Evans, Jorge had lived in California and got on well with everyone, including his comrades, of all ranks. He made life for the settlement folk much easier than might otherwise have been the case and interceded on their behalf with Lieutenant Marega (who also spoke fluent English) when necessary. For their part, the majority of the troops were decent young men, albeit cold, hungry, dirty, homesick and frightened, and recognised that the islanders were fellow human beings.

LISTENING-IN

The islanders knew something of what was happening beyond their shores as Ken Berntsen explained, *'following the lead of Nobby Clarke* [the islanders] *rigged improvised aerials to listen to the BBC World Service with small wireless sets and keep abreast of events. The method was quite simple really. All they did was run a piece of wire from the wireless to the main water supply pipe. This was made of galvanised metal and ran into the house from outside. These pipes usually entered the house somewhere high up, as there were storage tanks in the loft that have to be filled. Once all the locals were in the Big House, they got to know one of the guards* [Jorge] *who spoke good English. Ken recalled that this guard would listen to the BBC World Service and write down what the British were reporting, then compare it with the very different information coming out of Argentina. Apparently it upset him that his own Government was feeding them false information.'*

Initially the marine guards in the Big House did not observe the Falklands custom of removing their boots before going indoors. After a hard day in the pastures, boots can get pretty grubby. However, the servicemen were young and homesick and since Falklands ladies are well used to handling grumpy men of all ages, with or without rifles, so soon everybody in the Big House got along as well as could be expected. The state of the other houses after the surrender and evacuation can only be imagined.

TRAGEDY

On 19 May the SAS Regimental family suffered a terrible blow. A number of men were cross-decking - moving from ship to ship - by helicopter in readiness for further operations. It was a routine matter; a short Sea King flight, just minutes from launch to landing. At around 1910hrs, as it was getting really dark, a Sea King HC4 took

Captain Gavin John Hamilton who was killed on West Falkland whilst giving covering fire so his colleagues could withdraw.

off from HMS *Hermes* to fly some SAS troops to HMS *Intrepid*. The helicopter had two pilots and a crewman and twenty-seven men from 22 SAS including two attached personnel, one from the Royal Signals, the other from the RAF. The Sea King was also carrying a large amount of equipment, making it slightly over the maximum payload weight although as it was to be a short flight the pilot reportedly reduced the fuel load to reduce the overall weight. The helicopter took off in light winds and with a mild sea swell without trouble. When it was at about 300 feet the Sea King started to descend towards HMS *Intrepid*, loitering with minimum headway to make the landing easier. The crew and passengers heard a flat, distinct thump, apparently from above them, followed by another from the engine housing, directly above some of them. The Sea King dipped once then dived and within four seconds hit the water with considerable force, killing some of the occupants. Others were knocked unconscious but, by some miracle, nine men, including the three crewmen, managed to scramble out of the side door, fortunately kept open during the short flight more from instinct than intent. The helicopter then sank like the proverbial stone. The cause of the accident has never been fully identified; most accounts indicate bird strike, possibly an albatross. Eighteen SAS men, their attached RAF Forward Air Controller, his signaller, and the Royal Marine helicopter crewman were lost. The Regiment had not lost so many men at once since thirty-five died during Operation BULBASKET in France in 1944.

Seven men from D Squadron were killed in the helicopter crash, including five from 19 (Mountain) Troop. The Troop Commander, Captain Gavin John Hamilton was later to be killed on West Falkland by Argentinian commandos while covering the withdrawal of his three colleagues. (His signaller was wounded and captured, one of only two British PoWs; the other was an RAF pilot.) Captain Hamilton was awarded a posthumous Military Cross, based largely on reports from Argentinian troops who witnessed his actions. Indeed his Argentinian opponents recommended him for the highest possible award for valour but as no other British officer was present to witness his actions there was no possibility of him receiving a posthumous Victoria Cross.

In addition to these tragic losses the sheer success of the SAS raid on Pebble Island was to have further far-reaching and catastrophic consequences for the men and the ships of the British Task Force.

RIPOSTE

Back on Pebble Island the poor toilet conditions led to illness amongst the garrison. The Argentinians contacted the International Committee of the Red Cross, who in turn asked the British government to allow evacuation of sick and injured personnel from various locations, including Pebble Island. Ken Berntsen, recalled the arrival of, 'a large white Red Cross ship. I am guessing that this was the Polar supply vessel **ARA** *Bahia Paraiso*. It anchored in Elephant Bay and lots of supplies were offloaded by helicopter'. There was twist to this apparent humanitarian gesture. Despite the presence of an ICRC representative on board, the *Bahia Paraiso* carried more than food and medical supplies to the Falklands. It also transported, illegally, an ingenious land-based anti-ship missile system, designed to counter British naval gunfire support and radar picket vessels.

Two innovative *Armada* engineering officers and some hard-working NCOs had created the system. It consisted of a four-wheeled, flatbed trailer and five canister-mounted MM-39 missiles, the shipborne version of the Exocet. The trailer was fitted with a launch-platform from the frigate ARA *Guerrica* (damaged at South

ARA Bahia Paraiso *in Red Cross colours during the campaign.*

Georgia by two Royal Marines manning a Carl Gustav 84mm recoilless gun) and parts of the aiming system of an obsolete anti-aircraft gun. The trailer could carry two missile-canisters and launch them in a salvo along a fixed line. The target acquisition and homing system did not require cueing from an airborne platform. Ground-based radar could identify and track a target entering the missile engagement envelope, a narrow arc centred and extending for about twenty miles from the launch point; the homing radar was activated immediately prior to launch. The system was unloaded from the *Bahia Paraiso* at Stanley. An SAS observation post, probably inside a wreck in the harbour area, spotted this and reported it. The system was trundled out after last light each night and parked on a road east of Stanley, at a site named *Emplazamiento Berreta* by the CCM, to await the appearance of a British naval gunfire support vessel.

SEQUEL

The first launch from Berreta took place on 27/28 May (the Official History has 1-2 June), against British ships conducting a night bombardment of the airport area; one of the two missiles misfired and remained in the canister. The second missed, but was spotted, visually and on radar, and the emissions from the launch and guidance radars alerted the British to a new threat.

A second launch on 11/12 June resulted in one of the two missiles hitting HMS *Glamorgan*. The subsequent fire destroyed the ship's helicopter, killing fourteen men and injuring thirteen.

After the surrender, the fifth missile was found in a ditch near Stanley and photographed by Ewen Southby-Tailyour.

The fifth MM-39 canister in a ditch. Ewen Southby-Tailyour

The *Bahia Paraiso*'s visit to Elephant Bay had been agreed to and then plotted by the Task Force. As a precaution an SBS OP was established on Pebble Island to watch for signs of another launcher.[1]

The garrison of marines and naval air and groundcrew were far from harmless. They had a sense of duty and good reason to support their increasingly beleaguered comrades on the main islands, with whom they were still in contact by radio. Also someone in the Argentinian command had found a way of using the garrison to strike back at the British.

When the Argentinians realised the British were inserting Special Forces onto the Islands by using the radar shadow, the FAA established an arc of observation posts around the defended localities on East Falkland. The posts were manned by well-trained and highly motivated volunteer observers.

In 1982 Britain had long since discarded as outdated the notion of using observation posts for aircraft spotting, although, as noted above, the Royal Observer Corps remained in existence until 1992. However, with a large country and limited radar assets, the FAA had a similar auxiliary service, *la Red de*

ROA Op on the Malvinas.

Observadores del Aire (ROA - Network of Air Observers) part of the Airspace Control System. It was manned by volunteers, including radio hams, who are trained to report aircraft movements in their home territory. When the invasion of the Islands was announced, followed by the prospect of a British counter-invasion, Argentinians who had been associated in any way with the armed forces rushed to volunteer their services. The Observadores were no exception.

The CCM established ten observation posts, each manned by two men, plus a small command and communications team of four men, including the detachment commander, in the CICM. The FAA selected a reserve officer, Major Alfredo Ocampo, to form and command the detachment. He selected twenty-three observers from amongst the hundreds who volunteered. The ROA team became part of the *Grupo de Operaciones Especiales (GOE) de la Fuerza Aerea Isla Malvinas.*

The posts, call signs Mike One to Mike Ten, were in frontline positions around Fortress Stanley, with Mike One on Sapper Hill, south of the town. A further post, Mike Eleven, manned by FAA aircrew without Pucaras, was set up at Goose Green, and another was formed on Pebble Island and manned by Mentor aircrew, well-trained and experienced in ship and aircraft recognition, which was why they remained after the raid.

The post on Pebble Island was located on First Mountain, in a rough rock sangar[2].

The remains of the CANA aircrew Observation Post on First Mountain. Allan White

Manning it was an arduous task, especially for naval aircrew unused to working outdoors on windy and exposed hilltops in a South Atlantic autumn. They were to be amply rewarded for their boredom and discomfort just ten days after enduring the stinging humiliation of the SAS raid.

The FAA and the *Armada* had good reason to regard the British Pebble Island radar picket as a major threat to their air operations. The radar picket had originally consisted of single ship, the Type 22 frigate, HMS *Broadsword*, fitted with the point-defence Sea Wolf system. When she was reinforced by HMS *Coventry*, a Type 23 destroyer with a long-range Sea Dart system, the resulting 'combo' became a thorn in the side of the Argentinians, being instrumental in the destruction of several aircraft. For example, on 9 May HMS *Coventry* had probably contributed to the loss of two A-4C Skyhawks of Grupo 4 and the deaths of their pilots, Tenientes Casco and Farias, by Sea Dart. Later that day an *Ejercito* Puma helicopter was shot down over Choiseul Sound by a Sea Dart from *Coventry*, with the loss of three aircrew.

The radar picket 'combo' also irritated the Argentinian command in other ways. On 23 May RAF Harriers bombed Pebble Island airfield. The wrecked aircraft suffered even more damage and everyone received a severe fright. Apparently there had been intelligence indications of Argentinian aircraft or helicopter activity around the airfield. This was probably, Argentinian accounts differ, a FAA Twin Otter flying a casualty evacuation mission, a skilful piece of flying using one of the old airstrips on Elephant Beach. An Argentinian intelligence station, thought to have been *Seccion de Operaciones Electronicas 602*s at Stanley, intercepted some of the radio traffic associated with the air raid and correlated it to the radar picket combo, reinforcing the need to eliminate it once and for all.

The Argentinians were determined to mark their National Day, the 25th of May.

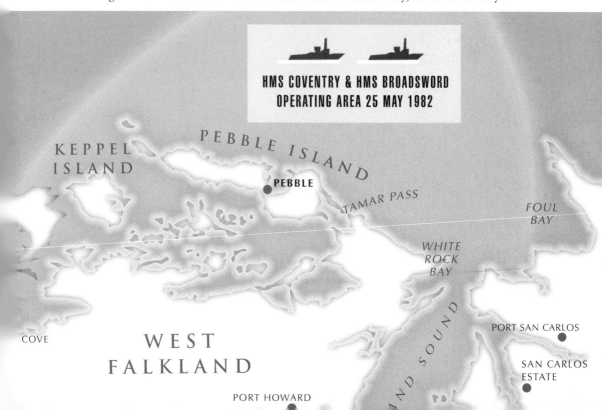

HMS COVENTRY & HMS BROADSWORD
OPERATING AREA 25 MAY 1982

KEPPEL
ISLAND

PEBBLE ISLAND

PEBBLE

TAMAR PASS

FOUL
BAY

WHITE
ROCK
BAY

PORT SAN CARLOS

COVE

WEST
FALKLAND

SAN CARLOS
ESTATE

SOUND

PORT HOWARD

A number of raids were planned, with the main effort against *Hermes* or *Invincible* using their last two remaining air-launched Exocets. Another attack would neutralise the combo, or at least divert the attention of the Task Force's anti-air warfare controller and of the radar operators on other ships.

A successful attack on the radar picket might serve to draw one or other of the aircraft carriers forward to cover any rescue operations - which is, in the event, exactly what happened. That would allow the second raid to mount Exocet launched strikes against the carriers.

On Sunday 23 May, as an innovative tactical 'force enhancement', the FAA started deploying its sole Hawker-Siddeley HS125 aircraft on pathfinder and decoy missions.[3] It was flown by senior officers and manned by others, including one acting as *Controlador Aereo Avanzado*. Their presence in the combat zone helped morale as casualties mounted in the Skyhawk squadrons, which lost 10 out of 36 pilots.

The National Day plan included two flights, each of three Skyhawks, to attack the combo. Argentinian intelligence, including data from SOE 602 had not revealed the identity of the ships, only that two different sets of emissions on slightly differing bearings were active in that general location.

On 25 May the combo was covering MV *Atlantic Conveyor*'s passage to San Carlos. It was spotted and reported to HQ in Stanley as 'a probable aircraft carrier' due the size of the radar image. It was to be attacked by two ANA Super Etendard aircraft, each armed with one Exocet missile, from BAN Rio Grande and escorted by Skyhawks acting as 'running interference' against the British Sea Harrier combat patrols. A KC130M Hercules tanker would refuel the Super Etendards.

ARGENTINIAN AIR ATTACK - 25 MAY 1982

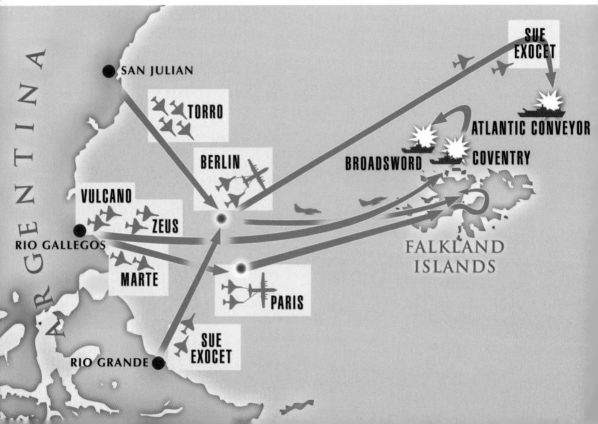

The observation post on First Mountain located the combo and alerted Stanley, which in turn alerted the mainland command centre. An Argentinian source recorded that;

> 'the British ships were under continuous surveillance by the Argentine observers placed on Isla Borbon, and they were found at 15 miles north of Pebble Island. Due to their relative proximity to the continent, it was decided that the air refuelling would not be necessary and, even more, all the Skyhawks would carry three bombs of 454 kgs (1,000 pounds), a war load normally not possible.'

As part of a wider plan which was directed against the Carrier Battle Group, a diversionary attack was launched against the combo. It consisted of two flights of Skyhawks; two (call sign *Marte*), from BAN Rio Gallegos, and four (call sign *Torro*) from BAM San Juan. Both refuelled en-route; *Torro* at point 'Berlin', *Marte* at 'Paris'. They over-flew San Carlos Water around noon but were badly mauled, losing three out of six aircraft. C-244 was lost to defensive fire and C-304 damaged. HMS *Coventry*, the Type 23 in the combo, heard the air attack alarm on the Anti-Air War net, and destroyed C-304 with a Sea Dart. That, and other losses, created a particular atmosphere which was later described by one FAA pilot. '*Before the radar picket mission we lost Palaver, Garcia and Lucero. Such an extraordinary performance created a "blood debt" within the FAA!*'

Skyhawk gun cameras film their attack runs against HMS Broadsword.

A further mission of six Skyhawks - '*Vulcano*' and '*Zeus*' flights, from Gallegos, accompanied much of the way by the HS125, call sign '*Ranquel*' by their commanding officer, *Vicecomodoro* Arturo Pereyra - was mounted against the combo in concert with the Super Etendard raid against the Carrier Battle Group.

Only two Skyhawks of each flight were able to reach the tanker point to refuel, however, and go on to press home the attack. Approaching the Falklands they peeled off from the HS125 and descended to low level for the run-in to the target area. *Coventry*'s radar picked them up at 140 miles but lost the image when they used terrain-masking to cover their approach. The mission-planners ELINT was excellent. Flying extremely low and initially masked by the hills on West Falkland, Keppel and Pebble Island, the Skyhawks managed to elude *Coventry*'s radar.

Vulcano flight - Captain Pablo Carballo (C-214) and Lieutenant Carlos Rinke (C-225) - attacked HMS *Broadsword*. Her radar acquired two targets and initiated an engagement with the Seawolf system. The British combat patrol pilots, Lieutenant Commander Neil Thomas and Lieutenant David Smith, were aware of the incoming aircraft, but were ordered to leave the area so that *Broadsword*'s Sea Wolf system would not lock-on to one of their Sea Harriers.

Just before the Sea Wolf system was ready to fire, the *Vulcano* aircraft, approaching in such close formation that they created a single radar image onto which the Sea Wolf system locked, became two as they separated for the final run-in. This confused the Sea Wolf computer which, at the critical moment 'crashed'. The launcher automatically slewed to its stowed fore/aft position, and was unable to be reset before the Skyhawks dropped their bombs. Only one bomb hit the ship but was dropped too low for the fuse to arm; it was operated by a small propeller in the nose, initiated when the bomb-release is operated. The bomb bounced off the sea, entered the side of the ship and travelled up through the flight deck, tearing the nose off a Lynx helicopter, on loan from HMS *Brilliant*, in the process, starting a fire. The bomb continued up and away from the ship and eventually landed harmlessly in the sea.

Zeus flight, Lieutenants Mariano Velasco (C-212) and Jorge Barrionuevo (C-207), were tracked by the radar of both ships. *Coventry* launched a Sea Dart but the Skyhawks evaded it. *Broadsword*'s Sea Wolf system locked on but again became confused. The operator over-rode the system and acquired the incoming Skyhawks visually and was ready to use manual control, using the TV-type camera on the mount. Now HMS *Coventry* appeared in the line of sight; apparently the 'gun-camera' tape shows this happening. One source claims no missile left its silo, another has *Coventry* hit by a Sea Wolf. Lieutenant Velasco stated afterwards that, 'Captain David Hart-Dyke, after having seen the attack performed by Carballo and Rinke, ordered the ship to manoeuvre so to protect - as he thought - the defenceless frigate by bravely putting his own ship between the damaged frigate and the new group of attackers when the Seawolf went off-line.' However, there was no time for the two ships' crews to identify a systems failure, report it internally then on the ship-to-ship anti-air warning frequency and for *Coventry*'s team to react, order a change of course and for the ship to respond.

The two A-4s were now only seconds away from *Coventry*. Lieutenant Velasco's bombs failed to release, but Barrionuevo's bomb release worked faultlessly. At 14.24 hrs HMS *Coventry* was struck by three 1,000lb bombs. Two exploded in the engine room machinery spaces, killing nineteen crewmen and causing a large fire. The ship eventually sank and now lies at 51 04'. 077 S/ 059 42'. 727 W.

All four Skyhawks returned to base safely, though Carballo's had been hit by gunfire from the *Broadsword*.

As *Coventry* was sinking one Super Etendard attacked *Atlantic Conveyor*, which was also sunk with loss of life and almost the entire stock of British helicopters. The other Etendard's missile disappeared; there are persistent claims by Argentinian sources that it hit *Hermes*.

In the words of Lieutenant (in 2006 *Vicecomodoro*) Pablo Marcos Rafael Carballo;

'May 25 1982 was a very special day [in many ways]... it was one more anniversary of our Homeland and we could celebrate it the best way: defending the most beautiful flag of the world. The second one was that a series of negative news [stories] had caused many people to lose their faith. The third one was that the whole world had started to talk about the Argentine pilots, and their Skyhawks .... that was very stimulating for us.'

HMS **Coventry** *after the attack.*

MV **Atlantic Conveyor** *after the attack.*

As a result of the raid and to avoid retribution on the observers on First Mountain, it was thought the SBS might exact revenge for the sinking of *Coventry*, the CANA mounted a daring long-range helicopter mission to evacuate them from Pebble Island. On 27 May Lieutenant Commander Norberto Barro, commanding 2nd Helicopter Squadron, was ordered to conduct the evacuation. The squadron was deployed at BAN Trelew, on the Atlantic coast, using its SH3 Sea King helicopters which it used to search for British submarines. The SH3s were far from ideal for a rescue mission as their fuselages were almost filled with dipping sonar and other anti-submarine warfare associated equipment. They were not fitted with electronic countermeasures (ECM) equipment and the navigation system was considered unreliable by the aircrew. The maximum speed was around 135 knots and the economical cruising speed very much lower. Their only strong points were their long range and some very experienced and highly motivated crews in addition to which they were the only aircraft available for a rescue mission. Being long-range naval helicopters they had large undercarriage sponsons which acted as floats.

Sea Kings 2-H-233 and 2-H-234 were selected for the mission. Lieutenant Commander Barro would fly H-233 with Lieutenant Guillermo Iglesias as second pilot and Senior Chief Petty Officer Beltrán Giqueaux as Loadmaster. Lieutenants Osvaldo and Iglesias Oscar Brandenburgo, with CPO Roberto Montani as Loadmaster flew H-334.

In order to give the helicopters greater endurance, the squadron's ground staff removed the anti-submarine equipment and any other items not required for an air evacuation and installed flexible fuel bladders and hand-pumps. Immediately before take-off the bladders were filled with fuel; at *Borbon* it would be transferred to the main tanks. The Sea Kings were also fitted with a very low frequency Omega Navigation system and

FAA Skyhawk pilots. www.skyhawk.com

Lt Barranoeva seated in his A-4C Skyhawk, points to the kill emblems which were credited to him for his attack on HMS Coventry and Brilliant.

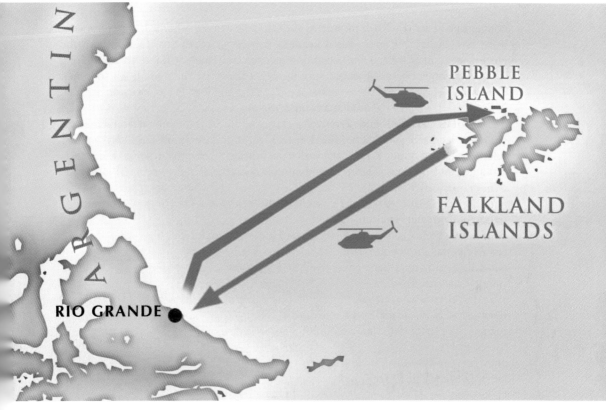

HELICOPTER RESCUE FLIGHT ROUTES

equipment associated with night vision for the pilots.

The Sea Kings arrived at BAN Rio Grande on 31 May, where H-233, was given a field-expedient camouflage scheme but the urgency of the rescue prevented the other from being repainted. The night vision equipment was tried but without much success. The aircrew met their PNA opposite numbers manning a Puma Search and Rescue helicopter. This would act as a navigation leader and radio relay station (rescue ship) for the first 120 miles of the outward leg of the mission. It would then return to base, refuel, and rendezvous with the Sea Kings for the final sector of the inward flight.

The three helicopters lifted off at 1400hrs the following day and headed east. The Puma left the formation at 1445hrs, and the Sea Kings landed on *Borbon* at 1725hrs, in the midst of worsening weather conditions. The aircrews supervised the refuelling, helped by despondent marines.

However, problems started to emerge when the hitherto reliable Omega failed. Nevertheless, at 1835hrs the Sea Kings took off for Rio Grande. Lieutenant Commander Barro had to fly higher than intended as the night vision was not working properly, while the second Sea King was able to continue flying at low-level. Those were not the only difficulties; both helicopters were flying some 600 pounds above their design payload, the fuel in the bladders was contaminated and there was a constant danger of icing. All went well, however, and the two Sea Kings were landed safely at 2200hrs. The crews and aircraft had conducted a remarkable long distance mission, operating close to the British radar, air patrols and missile umbrella of the Task Force.

At *Borbon* the Sea Kings were observed by the SBS observation post. The undercarriage sponsons were reportedly mistaken for missiles and reported as such. Someone in the British air or naval intelligence fraternity assessed them as being Argentinian Pescador (Kingfisher) anti-ship missiles, derivatives of the US Navy's Bullpup air-to-ground missile. The Pescador was not then in service. An attack by two or three SBS Sections, by then not required elsewhere, supported by naval gunfire support and Sea Harriers was planned - just in case- but in the event was not required.

In early June, Admiral Woodward had a final idea for establishing a forward operating base on Pebble Island. This was to install a company of RM Commandos on Pebble to ensure it was never used as a land-based Exocet launch site. Nothing came of that proposal.

Events elsewhere overtook those plans, however, and on June 14 the Argentinians surrendered after some bitter and costly fighting for the mountains which had formed the ring of defences surrounding Port Stanley.

EPILOGUE

Major Ewen Southby-Tailyour was one of a party who took the news of the surrender to various settlements on West Falkland by Wessex helicopter. The official herald was the commanding officer of the SBS, Major Jonathan Thomson. He was accompanied by his Second in Command, the Squadron Sergeant Major and some SBS minders. On the way they picked up the journalist Max Hastings and ITN newsman Michael Nicholson. The group flew to Pebble Island by way of Port Howard, Port Purvis House and Whale Bay. Flying towards Phillips Cove the Wessex pilot spotted a Land Rover and some figures on a ridge above the pond. The figures took cover behind the Land Rover and aimed their rifles at the descending helicopter. Once the aircraft had landed the armed men were quickly surrounded by the SBS marines and were found to be four Argentinian Combat Engineers, happy that the war was over.

Infanteria bring out their arms and ammunition for handover. Imperial War Museum FKD661(C)

Major Southby-Tailyour (third left), and a very happy Combat Engineer (second left), above Phillips Cove.

Imperial War Museum FKD661(C)

From left: Norman Morrison, Nobby Clark, Arina Berntsen and Griff Evans poses with the huge Union flag. Ewen Southby-Tailyour

They were preparing to destroy some tubes of Plastic Explosive, now no longer required as the surrender had been announced by radio. However, the 'demolition site' was on the general line of the cross-country route between the settlement and the 'hiding' place of the rubber boats, stored ready for a withdrawal to Port Howard.

The helicopter group continued on to the settlement and landed on an open space between the shearing shed and the Big House. There was no one in sight apart from some men below the House but as soon as the group started to walk towards them the entire pasture was suddenly ringed with Argentinian servicemen, not at all sure what to make of this sudden visit.[1] The delighted Islanders joined them; Griff Evans disappearing suddenly to return with a huge Union Jack. The Royal Marines party and islanders later inspected the airfield and its sad (and dangerous) relics before

The remnants of the raid as seen on 15 June by the Royal Marines contact team and the residents. The Pucara ejections seats had not been 'made safe' by the departing FAA groundcrew. Ewen Southby-Tailyour

The Coventry Memorial. R Evans

The Learjet Memorial. R Evans

A Mentor stands as a mute memorial to the folly of war. R Evans

returning to the settlement for a celebration. For them, and the Argentinian Marines, who were now starting to lay out their arms and ammunition for handover, the war was over.

Later, some SAS men returned to collect bergans, Klepper canoes and other items. Much later several memorials were erected on Pebble Island. One is for the men of HMS *Coventry*, another for the crew of an FAA Learjet. A third commemorates the SAS raid. Other, less formal memorials, are formed by the scattered remains of aircraft damaged or destroyed on the airfield. One lies elsewhere.

Mentor 411 was disabled during the raid. After the surrender it was protected from trophy-hunters by the islanders, particularly the Evans and Clarke children. In early 1983 the British Battlefield Clearance Team had listed all Argentinian weapons and major equipment found on the Islands, and identified items for retention or disposal. The Mentor was considered by RAF and FAA engineers to be restorable to display condition and it was allocated to the Royal Navy as a war-trophy. In June a RAF Chinook lifted the carcass onto the RFA *Sir Geraint*, which carried it to Marchwood Military Port, Southampton. Once unloaded it was dismantled by personnel from the Royal Navy's Mobile Aircraft Repair And Salvage Unit, who then moved the 'kit' to the Fleet Air Arm Museum, Yeovilton, where it was re-assembled and put on display in the Cobham Hall.

The Battlefield Clearance Team did not find a radar set or even the remains of one on Pebble Island. No record of a radar set on Pebble Island has ever been located. The Argentinian FAA's Historical Branch states, without qualification, that no radar was present at the time of the raid. The ELTA surveillance set may have been there

108

Above: The SAS Memorial. R Evans

Below and right: Corroding remains of the Skyvan and a Pucara stand as a reminder to Operation PRELIM. R Evans

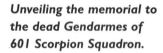

Unveiling the memorial to the dead Gendarmes of 601 Scorpion Squadron.

Argentine Memorial to the dead of the Malvinas conflict. HMS *Glamorgan* website

for a short period, landed from MV *Forrest* during its brief call on accompanied by the PNA cutter, on 28 April.[2] Another possible source of the solitary emission was a Neptune's surface search radar, during one of the last flights, south-west of the Islands. The Official History implies that there never was a set on Pebble Island.[3] The surviving residents have no recollection of anything like a radar set on the island during those troubled times.

Today Pebble Island is once more clean, green and serene. The Big House is now a guesthouse, Pebble Island Lodge, and is comfortable and hospitable. Its owners, Allan White and Jacqui Jennings and sheep farmers Raymond and Russell Evans are the only residents. They are alone with the wind, the sheep, the memories of departed friends and relatives, interred in the humble cemetery and of the dead, both British and Argentinian, commemorated by memorials and resting in war cemeteries or whose whereabouts are, to quote Rudyard Kipling, 'Known Unto God'.

Pebble Island will perhaps, never escape the fact that it was the scene of a spectacular and successful SAS raid. Nowadays, however, visitors to Pebble are always welcome, that is if they come unarmed and in peace.

NOTES

INTRODUCTION

1. Deeley, G, *Worst Fears Confirmed*, (London: Spellmount 2005) p.p. 255-258. In May 1945, Operation HERRING was mounted by the British/Italian No 1 (Italian) Special Air Service Regiment, against German and RSI (Italian Fascist) communications centres, and airfields in the Po Valley. The little-known No. 1 Italian SAS was raised in 1944 by British Intelligence officers, some of Italian descent, and manned by volunteers from the Italian Folgore (and later Nembo) Parachute Divisions. (There was to be a 2 ISAS, but the war ended before it was raised.) These were quite separate from the British SAS formations raised in Egypt and Algeria, but were raised under the same Middle East War Establishment as the original 1 SAS, which had been disbanded. The later 1 and 2 SAS were raised in the UK under new War Office WEs)

2. Reference to Admiral Woodward in Clapp, M and Southby-Tailyour, E, *Amphibious Assault Falklands*, (Barnsley: Pen & Sword/Leo Cooper, 1996) p. 69.

3. Website of HMS *Alacrity*; extracts from the ship's log, May 1982.

4. HMS *Sheffield*; sunk after being hit by an AM29 Exocet missile launched from a CANA Super Etendard fighter-bomber, cued by a Lockheed SP2H Neptune MPA orbiting south-west of West Falkland.

THREAT

1. *Amphibious Assault Falklands*, p. 69
2. *ibid*, pp. 56, 79
3. *Reasons in Writing*, Southby-Tailyour, E, *(Barnsley: Pen & Sword, 2003) p. 313*
4. *Author conversations* with 'Esteban', summer 2005 - spring 2006.

PEBBLE ISLAND

1. *Falkland Islands Shores*, Southby-Tailyour, E, (London: Conway Maritime, 1985) p.105

OCCUPATION

1. *Separata No. 20*, Department of History, Argentinian Marine Corps, 1997 p.10
2. *ibid*, p.11

DEFENCE

1. '*Buzos*'. These are the *Armada*'s only Naval (as opposed to *Infanteria*) Special Forces unit, the *Agrupacion de Buzos Tdcticos* (Tactical Diver Group), part of the *Fuerza de Submarinos* - submarine force. The group was formed in 1953 and trained by former members of the Italian Navy's famous '*Decima Mas*' (Tenth Motor Boat Squadron), which included frogman-parachutists in its ranks. The ABT is based near the submarine force in Mar del Plata Naval Base. Buzos have six main roles:

a. SUBSUNK assistance (equivalent to the Royal Navy Submarine Parachute Assistance Group), working with the *Fuerza de Submarinos* Search and Rescue Group, including the Submarine Rescue Ship.

b. Defensive Combat Swimmers checking for, and then disarming and removing, limpet mines from ships and naval installations.

c. Beach and seaway reconnaissance ahead of amphibious landings.

d. Maritime Counter-Terrorists missions.

e. Offensive Combat Swimmers placing limpet mines on ships and naval installations

f. Small scale raiding; including manning OPs, conducting Close Target Reconnaissance, mounting raids or assassinating key enemy personnel, or acting as Pathfinders and guides for *Infanteria*

Amphibious Commando units. Many Buzos are parachutists, both free-fall (HALO, HAHO and LALO) and static-line; for landing on land in battle order, or into the sea, lakes, lagoons and rivers in swimming gear (SCUBA equipment and wet-suits). In the Falklands the *Buzos*, if deployed could have used the PNA Skyvans for free-fall or static line jumps. The BT could be delivered into operational areas by either the SSCs or the SSK, Armada Fast Attack Craft or the smaller Mantilla class patrol cutters of the Prefectura such as the Iguazu. Other means of delivery included Rigid Raiders, and small cutters, rubber boast and canoes. Also light amphibious civilian aircraft, ATUFT such as De Havilland Canada (DHC) Beaver and Otter floatplanes. They were widely used in Patagonia and Tierra del Fuego to transport fishing parties and easily acquired by the Argentine Navy or LADE as ATUFT and can land and take-off from areas such Big Pond as did the FIGAS Beavers before 1979.

SPECIAL FORCES

1. In 1987 renamed Special Boat Service

2. MAWC; mainly involved in training RM Mountain Leaders; three grades - ML1, ML2, ML3.

3. Captain Bell, bilingual in Spanish and English, served as an interrogator and translator for much of the campaign. The RAFVR and Territorial Army had some competent Spanish-speaking reservist interrogators but declined to mobilise them, despite the fact that the RAFVR ones could be easily mobilised. 'FOB watching' was carried out on various islands including Pebble Island. There are conflicting views about the time of insertion of that patrol. One account (Connor, Ken, *Ghost Force, The Secret History of the SAS* p.259), has the SBS offered the option of setting up Op PRELIM but could not do the task (this author's emphasis). This probably means all sections were committed elsewhere, or that there was an OP already on Pebble Island, but - and this makes much sense - its presence could not be revealed in case the raid went wrong and its crew were compromised thus depriving the Task force of any eyes on the airfield and bay. It would also have alerted the Argentinians to OPs on candidate FOB islands.

4. Major Ewen Southby-Tailyour mentions in 'Falkland Islands Shores' replenishing the OP team (which, after the raid, spotted the hospital ship in Elephant Bay; see Chapter 8 Aftermath) at the time of surrender, and Sam Miller, the farmer on Keppel Island, recalled (2005) being told after the surrender that a 'Special Forces' patrol landed there by canoe; it may have gone from there to Pebble. Maybe someday an accurate account will be available!

5. See HMS *Ardent* website for log entries during and after the attack on *Sheffield*.

RECONNAISSANCE & PLANNING

1. Bergans, not 'bergens'. Named after the designer and manufacturer. Ole F. Bergan invented the pack frame and already, in 1908, he had patented the frame carrying system under the trade name 'Bergans'. This is the same fundamental idea on which the construction of today's modern backpacks is based. The Norwegian Army has used Bergans backpacks since 1913.

RAID

1. According to the *Fuerza Aerea Argentina*'s Historical Branch, contacted in January 2006, there was no ammunition on the airfield on the night of the raid. It is not clear whether they were referring just to FAA ammunition, or to that of any service; CANA/Marines, etc, as Argentinian service sources rarely cover each other's activities! The records of the Royal Army Ordnance Corp's EOD team on Pebble Island remained closed at the time of writing, so it is not clear what was in the settlement. Possibly only 7.62mm ammunition used for the Mentor's guns and the Marines' small arms and the 500 plus 75mm recoilless rifle rounds. Some of these were fired for practice as the

crews were not too familiar with the weapons and had never fired them in the field, only on a range, from robust, well-prepared and maintained emplacements.

2. Some accounts of the raid state, or at least imply, that when the SAS returned fire they either killed or wounded one or some Argentinian Marines. At the time of writing no record of any Marine being killed or wounded in the action has been located. There is certainly no mention of any casualties, fatal or otherwise, in Separata No.20.

AFTERMATH

1. The Junta had disbanded most of the few Argentinian SF units to prevent them being used to stage a *coup d'etat*, a wise precaution as later, personnel of the Commando unit re-activated for ROSARIO attempted to do just that – twice.

2. An SAS strike on the main base area in Stanley was apparently considered but rejected in favour of reconnaissance, considered to be a better use of scarce resources.

3. Scorpion Squadron http://ar.geocities.com/laperlaaustral/gendarmeria.htm. The Scorpion Squadron was considered by the GN to be Special Forces, albeit with a limited role: it was a highly specialised urban and rural anti-terrorist tracking, stalking and assault team. If deployed properly it might have caused problems for British special forces OPs deployed around the Argentinian perimeter.

4. *Separata* No. 20, p. 37.

5. *ibid.*

6. *ibid.*

RIPOSTE

1. The location of the OP had not been identified at the time of writing but is thought to have been in rough country northwest of Elephant Beach.

2. By a quirk of history there were precedents for OPs on Pebble Island. Coast-watching OPs had been a way of life on the Falklands for many years, mainly to do with reporting merchant shipping for commercial reasons.

   Naval OPs had been established when war broke out in 1914. They were, in part, based on the idea of an Imperial chain of Sea Scouts and Coast Watchers submitted to the Admiralty in 1911 by General Sir Robert Baden-Powell, founder of the Boy Scout movement. The Falklands chain was manned by Settlement Volunteers and was soon put to the test.

   On the morning of 8 December 1914, a Coast-Watcher manning the Look-Out Hill OP south of Stanley spotted the smoke of the Imperial German Pacific Squadron heading for Stanley. Unbeknown to the Germans a strong RN flotilla was in Stanley harbour, hunting for the Squadron after it had annihilated a British force in the Battle of Coronel (1 November 1914.) The Germans intended to refuel in Stanley, using force majeur, not cash, – and the rest is history.

   Prior to the Second World War the Chiefs of Staff Committee in London were preoccupied with Imperial defence in the face of emergent and belligerent powers in Italy, Germany and Japan. An early move, in 1925, was to set up the Royal Observer Corps, and a similar idea was mooted for coast-watching, including mine-laying.

   Steps were taken to initiate some sort of war-plan in all colonies and dependent territories, including the Falklands. Not only was Argentina growing increasingly Germanophile but in 1938 the Nazis sponsored an unusual (and still not fully-explained) Antarctic expedition. It was a joint venture between the German Society of Polar Research and Lufthansa, and was based on a cargo ship, the *Schwabenland*, equipped with a large catapult for launching Dornier Do 15 Wal seaplanes. The expedition claimed some 400,000 square miles of Antarctic territory for the Reich, to be called Neu Scwhabenland, and lying about 1,000 kms south-east of the South Sandwich Islands. The venture was widely reported in British newspapers, and alerted the Admiralty to a possible wartime threat to whaling and merchant shipping in the South Atlantic from cruisers or U-boats. Not so much from any base in the Antarctic, but one established on the defenceless Falklands, seized possibly with help from the Argentinians. (The Germans did in fact use remote islands such as Gough and Kerguelen in the Southern Ocean as refuges for the commerce raiders *Pinguin* and *Atlantis*, and contemplated using them for U-boat bases.) On the Falklands a simple coast-watching service equipped with radios was quickly activated. On Pebble Island that involved three residents; Owen McPhee, Tommy Anderson and Jack Ashley - all members of the Settlements Volunteers. Marble Mountain North Peak had been selected for the site of an OP, built from rocks and corrugated iron; Marble Shanty equipped for semi-permanent residence, and fitted with a petrol-engine electricity generator and a refurbished stable. Once news of the outbreak of war was received in Stanley and transmitted to the other settlements the three young men travelled to Marble Shanty on horseback and established a rotating watch system. Sightings were reported by radio to Pebble Island settlement, and relayed to Stanley. The men spent twelve weeks keeping a 24-hour watch from the mountaintop. Each four-hour watch began after a horse-ride to the top of the mountain from Marble Shanty, followed by an eight-hour break before repeating the process. Hauling radios of that era to the top of the mountain was no mean feat. They were powered by six-volt accumulators and acid-filled glass containers, in general use before the advent of large dry batteries. The accumulators were re-charged in the Shanty and transported to the OP on horseback, balanced on the saddle in front of the rider. Owen said that several days later the front of the riders' trousers disintegrated from acid spilled from the batteries during the journeys. Each four-hour watch began by catching, feeding and harnessing a wilful Island horse, collecting an accumulator from the charging-shed, then a cold ride to the OP; a hard, lonely and boring way to serve one's country.

3. The HS125 flights were augmented by those of the Fenix (Phoenix) Squadron. This was a flight of commandeered civilian Learjet executive aircraft, mainly manned by retired aircrew. Fenix was based at BAM Trelew, home to the FAA's Canberra bomber squadrons. The unarmed Learjets simulated Canberra raids in hope of being picked up by British radar and thus divert the British CAPs, allowing the Skyhawks and Daggers to attack the Task Force. At a safe distance the Learjets would turn and head for base. If nothing else the Fenix operations forced the British to scramble their CAPs frequently thereby increasing the pressure on air and groundcrew, airframes and fuel. On a number of occasions one of the Learjets was flown by Tito Withington. He was born in Córdoba of British parentage, and during the Second World War was one of several hundred Argentinians who served in the RAF. Tito served with 625 Squadron, flying Lancaster bombers from RAF Kelstern, near Grimsby. He was an intensely patriotic Argentinian, and when the call went out for volunteers for Fenix could not resist. He was 60 years, and, happily, survived his second war unharmed.

EPILOGUE

1. The actual head-count of Argentinian personnel amazed the British; it was over eighty men, many in poor condition. (Argentinian figures differ; eighty-four is a favoured figure!)

2. *Official History*, Freedman, Sir L, (London: Routledge, 2005) p.179

3. *ibid*, p.431

SELECT BIBLIOGRAPHY

Michael Clapp, *Amphibious Assault: Falklands* (Barnsley Pen & Sword/Leo Cooper, 1996)

Jeffrey Ethell, Alfred Price *Air War: South Atlantic* (London Sidgwick and Jackson, 1984)

Lawrence Friedman, *The Official History of the Falklands Campaign*, (London, Routledge, 2005)

Max Hastings, Simon Jenkins, *The Battle for the Falklands* (London 1984)

Martin Middlebrook, *The Falklands War 1982.* (London, Penguin, 2001)

Martin Middlebrook, *The Argentinian Fight for the Falklands.* (Barnsley, Pen & Sword, 2003)

Ruben O. Moro, *The History of the South Atlantic Conflict* (London, Praeger, 1989)

Eugene Rasor, *The Falklands/Malvinas Campaign* (Greenwood Press, 1991)

Peter Ratcliffe, *Eye of the Storm: 25 Years in Action with the SAS.* (London, O'Mara, 1997)

Ewen Southby-Tailyour, *Reasons in Writing.* (Barnsley Pen & Sword/Leo Cooper, 2003)

Nicholas Van Der Bijl, *Argentine Forces in the Falklands* (MAA No. 250) (London, Osprey 1986)

Sharkey Ward, *Sea Harrier Over the Falklands*, (London, Orion Paperbacks, 1993)

Admiral Sandy Woodward, et al, *One Hundred Days*, (London, HarperCollins, 1992)

IN SPANISH

Separata No 20; Borbon; Equipo de Combate Marega; (Buenos Aires, Departamento de Historia del Comando de la Cuerpo de Infanteria Marina Armada Arrentina, 1997)

WEBSITES

www.ara.mil.ar (*Official Argentinian Navy site.*)

www.avionesdemalvinas.com

www.btinternet.com/broadsword82/

www.britains-smallwars.com/Falklands/sas.htm

www.ejercito.mil.ar (*Official Argentinian Army site.*)

www.helis.com/stories/borbon.php

www.fuerzaaerea.mil.ar/conflicto/operaciones_aereas.html (*A useful day-by-day resume of events; in the official Argentinian Air Force site.*)

www.gendarmeria.gov.ar (*Official Argentinian Gendarmeria Nacional site.*)

www.malvinas.com

www.naval-history.net

www.prefecturanaval.gov.ar (*Official Argentinian Coastguard site. Only the Spanish/Castellano version has much on the Malvinas/Falklands campaign.*)

www.sama82.org

Note: some Spanish designations have not been translated in the text, as their meaning is self-evident.
    Eg Centro de Información y Control

GLOSSARY

AAA	Anti-Aircraft Artillery
Armada	Argentinian Navy
ARA	Armada Republica Argentina; equivalent of 'HMS'
AWACs	Airborne Warning & Control aircraft
BAM	Base Aero Militar – Argentinian air force or army airfield
BAN	Base Aero Naval – Argentinian naval airfield
Buzos Tacticos	Armada SF.
CANA	Comando Aviacion Naval Argentina; equivalent of Fleet Air Arm
CAP	Combat Air Patrol; British/NATO term for standing defensive counter-air mission over key points or areas
CICM	Centro de Información y Control Malvinas Control & Information Centre, Stanley
COMIL	Comando Militar, Argentinian Military Command, part of the *Junta*'s apparatus; form of Joint Chiefs of Staff.
Cross-decking	transfer of personnel and stores between ships by helicopter, highline or small craft
DSASG	Director Special Air Service Group. In 1982 Brigadier (later Sir) Peter de la Billiere, DSO, MC
EA	Ejercito Argentina-Army
ELINT	Electronics Intelligence; collection and assessment of electronic emanations such as radar; now classed as RADINT (Radar Intelligence) ELINT is gathered by ground, airborne, surface and sub-surface platforms, and via satellites.
FAA	Fuerza Aérea Argentina air force.
FI	Falkland Islands
FIC	Falklands Islands Company
FIG	Falkland Islands Government
FIGAS	Falkland Islands Government Air Service
FOB	Forward Operating Base
GN	Gendarmería Nacional de Argentina - state rural and border police force. The original GN Malvinas detachment was reinforced with an ad-hoc SF unit after Operation Prelim, the Escuadron Alacran de la Compania de Tropas Especiales 601 de Gendarmería Nacional (Scorpion Squadron, 601 SF Company)
Infanteria	used throughout to denote the Cuerpo de Infanteria de Marina: 'Marine Infantry'; Argentinian Marines; part of the Armada. This force is modelled on the United States Marine Corps. In 1982 it had two Fleet Marine Forces, each with one infantry regiment of three battalions: infantry companies were numbered within the regiment, not by battalion, hence G,H and I Companies, 3d Battalion, (see text).

Junta	Argentinian Junta Militar, three senior officers with little grasp of politics or diplomacy, controlling their nation through coercion and fear
Kelp	Seaweed growing in long fronds, once harvested and burnt for fertiliser, a big export in bygone days, hence name 'Kelpers' for islanders.
LADE	Lineas Aereas del Estado; Argentinian government airline, part of FAA; before the invasion it operated a twice–weekly service between mainland Argentina and Stanley airport. It had a hangar and offices at Stanley airport; the staff lived in the town and have been accused of spying. Most flights carried several extra aircrew, ostensibly to buy off-duty whisky at the FIC stores. The F-27 Friendship aircraft used for the service may have been fitted for covert photography. Not long before the invasion the LADE manager, Vicecomodoro [equates to RAF Wing Commander] Wilson Pedrozo, showed a party of 'FAA aircrew' around a number of beaches and other areas close to Stanley.
LST	Landing Ship, Tank
LS	Landing Site; used here for both aircraft/helicopter and shipping locations
LVPT-5	Landing Vehicle, Personnel, Tracked; Model 5. US-built amphibious landing tractor
LUP	Lying-Up Position, see OP, below
MPA	Maritime Patrol Aircraft: RAF Nimrod, Argentinian Neptune
SRMPA	short range maritime patrol aircraft for inshore operations]
Midshipman	used here in place of Guardiamarina; a junior Marine officer; equates to 2/Lt
NGS	Naval Gunfire Support,
NGLO	Naval Gunfire Liaison Officer; Artillery specialist on board ship providing NGS
NGFO	Naval Gun Fire Observer; Artillery fire controller on land or inshore, directing NGS
NP8901	Naval Party 8901; official designation of the Falkland Islands Royal Marine garrison, repatriated to Britain by way of Montevideo after the Argentinian invasion
OP	Observation Post. Special Forces ones are usually near a LUP, which provides a resting place; off-watch personnel can provide cover for observers
PNA	Prefectura Naval Argentina; Coast Guard, in times of transition to war/war under operational control of the Armada
POA	Puestos de Observadores del Aire equivalent of WWII Royal Observer Corps posts
RALONGS	Royal Artillery Liaison Officer, Naval Gunfire Support; staff appointment within the 3 Commando Brigade HQ. Co-ordinates the work of all NGLOs and NGFOs and RN and RM staff, and sometimes Army and RAF mission planners

RFA	Royal Fleet Auxiliary; UK civilian-manned supply and logistics shipping service
ROA	Red de Observadores del Aire. (Air Observers Network) same as Royal Observer Corps.
SF	Special Forces
Stanley	Port Stanley, capital of the Falkland Islands, Puerto Argentina to the CCM
Stone Frigate	Naval land base
TACEVAL	Tactical Evaluation; RAF/NATO test of an air station's war-readiness
TASMO	Tactical Air Support of Maritime Operations: air force support to naval operations
TELs	Missile Transporter-Erector-Launcher vehicles
TF	Task Force; grouping of military/naval forces under one commander for a specific operation
TG	Task Group; component of a TF organised by the CTF.
TU	Task Unit: component of a TG organised by the CTF.
VYCA	Vigilancia y Control Areo: FAA Surveillance and Air Traffic Control radar system

INDEX

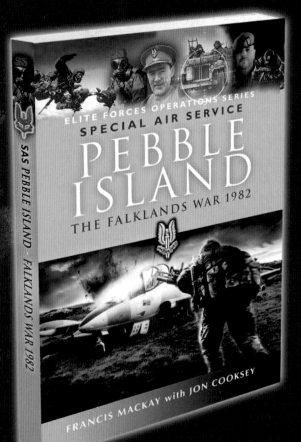

COLLECT THE SPECIAL OPERATIONS SERIES

SPECIAL AIR SERVICE

PARACHUTE REGIMENT

ROYAL MARINE COMMANDOS